Grief Quest

Donated to
SAINT PAUL PUBLIC LIBRARY

Grief Quest

MEN COPING WITH LOSS

Robert J. Miller
with Stephen J. Hrycyniak

Saint Mary's Press
Christian Brothers Publications
Winona, Minnesota

Genuine recycled paper with 10% post-consumer waste. Printed with soy-based ink.

The publishing team included Carl Koch, development editor; Laurie A. Berg, copy editor; Lynn Dahdal, production editor; Hollace Storkel, typesetter; Cindi Ramm, art director and cover designer; cover photo and photos on pages 15 and 69, Tom Lowes; pre-press, printing, and binding by the graphics division of Saint Mary's Press.

Printed in the United States of America

Printing: 9 8 7 6 5 4 3 2 1

Year: 2007 06 05 04 03 02 01 00 99

ISBN 0-88489-597-1

Dedication

To my father, Robert J. Miller,
    a gentle man of quiet strength and faith,
    committed, responsible, yet fun-loving,
    whose strengths laid the foundation for all I do and am
        today,
    whose embrace I eagerly await once again
    when my own earthly journey (griefquest) is completed.

To the four Miller brothers,
    Don, Ernie, Ray, Louie,
    priests and religious, cousins, writers,
    men of God, inspirations, friends.

To all men on the journey in the world today
    those wounded and grieving,
    lost and searching,
    growing and learning,
    seeking and finding,
    being saved, transformed, and healed.

To the man whose life makes all our quests worthwhile,
    Jesus of Nazareth.

Contents

Acknowledgments

My good friend Steve Hrycyniak and I first realized the need for and vision of *GriefQuest* in early 1995. Though originally we intended to write it together, circumstances were such that I became the primary author, and Steve became an invaluable touchstone and support for me. I thank him for his encouragement, advice, inspiration, research, and affirmation—and for being a true friend when I needed one the most.

Carl Koch from Saint Mary's Press saw value and worth in this manuscript three years after its initial release, and has worked hard to have it republished here in 1999. My deep thanks to him and his wife, Joyce, for believing in me and this work.

The men who originally shared their stories with me are each unique and special. I appreciate greatly the time they took to share their griefquests and the effort they made to open up their lives so that other men might be touched. Thanks ever so much to Cardinal Joe Bernardin, Linus Mundy, Abbot Lambert, Jack, Ken, Chip, Steve, Neil, and all the others!

I would like to publicly acknowledge the men who have touched and walked with me along my own faith journey. Some of these men have had a larger role and impact than others, but all have left footprints etched in my soul as their paths crossed mine. My own griefquest, and any spirituality and maturity I do have, is indebted to them: Mike Miller (my brother), John Harvey, Fred Saucedo, Pat Reeks, Joe Menke, John Tupper, Father Colman, Mike Butler, Steve Palmer, Bob Marnell (and his sons Bobby, Mike, Steve, and Mark), and my former Redemptorist confreres both living (Pete Schavitz, Dick Thibodeau, Henry Sattler, Art Rossie, Bob Oelerich) and deceased (Dick Hoffman, Jim Bohr, Bill Nugent).

Ad multos annos to all of you!

Foreword

The grieving mode keeps us out of the fixing mode. The grieving mode keeps us beyond the explaining mode. The grieving mode makes the way of blaming useless and counterproductive. The grieving mode submerges us into a world deeper than words or control. It is a way of hoping without specific plans. It is a way of believing without focusing on an idea. It is a way of loving that is greater than loving any particular object.

Grieving is not just something that we do on sad occasions. It is a mode of existence that agrees to carry the sadness of things without denying or dismissing the pain as an accident. It is a way of living that incorporates dying. It is a way of remembrance that refuses to forget. It is not a maudlin, depressed, or self-pitying thing, but a way of "compassion" that makes room for everything and holds on to nothing. Tears stream down the cheek to make room for more inside the eyes.

No wonder that Jesus cried at the presence of death (John 11:35) and as he looked over the city of lost opportunity (Luke 19:41). No wonder he named this mode "blessed" and promised comfort in his second description of happiness (Matthew 5:4). No wonder saints like Francis and Clare spent days and nights in "holy tears." Lamentation is a way out, a way through, a way into the holy mystery of things. It is the only human emotion that becomes the name of a book in the Bible.

It is hard to cry when you are young—and a man. It slows you down. It allows the wrong questions. It offers the wrong answers. It lets others in. It keeps you too close to what matters, to your true self, and probably to God. It seems to make sense for young men not to cry—to manage, fix, and think instead. But soon the patterns are in place, and the young men have become old men—and human culture has been formed—without wisdom.

I am convinced after twenty-five years in ministry that much that passes as strong opinion and anger is really grief disguised.

Much that passes as self-protection and fear is really grief denied. Much that passes as detachment and letting go is a grief so deep that there is no room for connection. Much that is done in the name of justice and peace proceeds from a well of tears and sadness. Much that is service and compassion comes from learning to cry without shame. I do not know which comes first—worship or tears—but I do know that each is a doorway to the other.

I wonder if we can yet recover tears as a way of wisdom and even a way of prayer. Bob Miller is surely laying the foundation and offering the freedom for such a way in this quite wonderful book. He leads us on a path that could end up being much more revolutionary than many teachings on nonviolence, forgiveness, and self-help.

Men will likely continue to resist and resent the world of grieving until they learn to do it in their own masculine, and still messy, way. Men will avoid and laugh at the way of tears until they see that it is the grounding of every revolution. It is the way of the prophets who taught Israel how to groan and lament their servitude. If there is no groaning, there is no liberation—only numbness and nihilism. Without pathos ("emotional suffering" in Greek), there is only a-pathy.

I doubt whether war could be so easily taught once men learn how to cry. I doubt whether incest or rape could be done by a man of tears. I doubt whether the whole system would work—this buying and selling thing that is destroying the temple—if men could only lament. This is no soft and sensual path—except in the sense that matters. This spirituality, this gift of tears, is the stuff of a whole new world.

Richard Rohr, OFM
Albuquerque, New Mexico

Introduction

Until you have cried, you do not know God.
                —Saint Ephraem, Syrian Father of the Church

He who has no time to mourn has no time to mend.
                                    —Unknown poet

In August 1967, a great man died. No politicians or world leaders attended the funeral, for his greatness was not in power, prestige, or position but in the value and significance the man held for his seventeen-year-old son. I was that seventeen-year-old son. It took me nearly twenty years to completely and fully mourn my father's loss and to acknowledge the positive impact he had on my life. I received virtually no help along the way—mainly because there were no mentors for me to turn to, because I wasn't able to receive or look for help, and because I didn't know myself what to do with what I felt inside. Thus, my own quest for inner peace with my father involved nearly twenty years of wandering and silent mourning. This book is the book I wish I had had a chance to read during those long years. When my good friend Steve Hrycyniak and I first conceived the idea for this book early in 1995, it immediately triggered a deep and resonant chord in me. A book needed to be written *by* men, *for* men, *about* how men grieve and why they can't grieve. Too many grieving men are wandering this world not knowing where to go or how to mourn, wondering if *they* are the only ones feeling so lonely and lost.

Both Steve and I knew that men would never pick up this book to begin with unless it were *not* clinical or "preachy," but down to earth and basic, filled with examples and stories of men who had faced grief and loss and "survived." Thus, personal stories of other men are the very heart of this book—stories of ordinary men, stories of a few prominent men, but all stories of hurting and grieving men. The stories of these brothers in God are the best teachers and carry the greatest wisdom of this book.

The book's title is significant. The search for healthy masculine ways to grieve is indeed a *quest*. Dealing effectively with the chaos and turmoil of grief can never be done in an organized, methodical pattern. I doubt there is one single effective male way of grieving losses. Rather, men today are learning together step-by-step how to grieve effectively. We are breaking new ground daily, questing and searching for knowledge about ourselves and our roles, images, and relationships in our fast-changing modern society. A man's *griefquest* is a personal search for inner peace and healing amid grief and loss—and it is a sacred, life-changing journey, no matter how long it takes.

GriefQuest is written for men and the women who love and care about them. Men (and women) need a book written by men that helps make sense out of the unique challenges that grief and loss force on men today. Although in *GriefQuest* we have intentionally focused on material written by men, this by no means is intended to downplay the wisdom and healing that women bring to men's lives. A woman's wisdom, strength, and balance is absolutely essential for any man seeking wholeness and peace. Likewise, despite the hurts done to women by broken men through the generations, I believe that no woman has anything to fear from a truly empowered and healthy male.

Last, I (and Steve) have conceived and written this book out of Christian foundation and background. As a Catholic priest of twenty-two years (and Steve is a Ukrainian deacon), I am proud to profess the debt I owe to Jesus Christ for what he has done in my life. Although faith and spirituality are absolutely key to any completely successful griefquest, *GriefQuest* is not a specifically "Christian book." The wisdom of Jesus and the Christian heritage are certainly spoken about in this book, but the focus is primarily *the common pains and griefs, strengths, and wisdom all men share together*—despite differences in faith or belief.

As we begin this griefquest journey, I do not pretend to have all the answers about men's grief, but I will offer whatever wisdom I have learned. Through the shared experiences of the men you will soon meet in these pages, I feel confident we can all come to a new level of peace, understanding, healing, and maybe even transformation!

Grief and loss from a man's point of view

Two of our "brothers" and their grief

During World War I, while stationed in France, a hard-punching young American boxer aspiring for greatness broke both his hands. His doctor and manager told him that he would never be able to realize his dream of becoming a heavyweight boxing champion because his hands were simply too brittle. But history relates a different ending to this story.

That young man took his "loss" and turned it into his greatest asset—he became a master of the art of self-defense, one of history's most scientific and skillful boxers. Because of his skill and technique, he was eventually able to enter the ring and defeat the legendary Jack Dempsey, becoming heavyweight champion of the world. Gene Tunney's victory was not just in the ring—it was dramatic victory over a uniquely masculine tragedy and loss. It was loss, pain, and grief turned into *glory*.

In 1992, Fr. Lambert Reilly was a Benedictine monk well known for his spirituality and retreats, some given around the world to groups such as Mother Teresa's nuns. In that year he discovered he had colon cancer and needed surgery followed by chemotherapy. He writes of the dramatic impact the experience had on his whole life:

> My hair thinned. I was frequently so sick from diarrhea and vomiting. During this time I kept going—doing things, even going to Canada for a retreat right after one treatment. But I couldn't bounce around like I used to. I had to say no to requests, which was something new to me. I didn't have any other option. How this affected me was strange. Spiritually I began to wish that God would call me home. Emotionally I was up and down. Psychologically I was mixed-up. It was so sudden, so new, so different. What did it mean?
>
> I had been a person who was always very forthright—I said what I thought. But this experience somehow told me there were *other* thoughts beyond mine. . . . I didn't have to

push mine so much, and I could allow more for others. The whole experience mellowed me.

The only thing in life that is truly supernatural is suffering. Suffering changes us. Change can either be for the better or the worse. I think my suffering was for the better. . . . The cancer nudged me closer to seeing like God does.

Perhaps God indeed was preparing Father Lambert to see differently, because two years after the surgery his Benedictine community elected him archabbot of his monastery. As 1996 began, Archabbot Lambert remained in good health, admitting freely that "the whole experience prepared me for the job I have now." The archabbot's sudden cancer changed him deeply, and all the grief was not in vain. His griefquest prepared him for the next unexpected step in his religious life—leadership in the church and community.

What is this thing called grief?

Learning a new language

Grief. The word itself is frightening to the majority of men. The mere thought of being forced to deal with death, loss, tragedy, pain, failure, or disaster may seem beyond our grasp. In general, we men are not comfortable looking into ourselves. We avoid that unknown inner world where everything is not organized, efficient, productive, or positive. What makes the topic of grief so disconcerting is the simple fact that it forces us into a hidden realm of our being where we are no longer "in control." Grief confronts us where we are most vulnerable and where we often have little experience or knowledge.

Because of this, we men must begin a griefquest to get in touch with a reality alien to many of us. Because we are not instinctively in contact with our feelings or emotions, this is a foreign world for us. Identifying and recognizing specific feelings as "grief feelings" can be as strange as learning a new language. It requires a new vocabulary, complete with idioms and nuances, as well as a new depth of awareness and perspective on personal experiences. For men willing to learn the "language" of grief, we commence our griefquest now by explaining what types of feelings grief may include.

Grief can include feelings of . . .

◆ intense mental anguish or "heaviness"
◆ acute sorrow and sadness
◆ mourning and lamenting
◆ anger, hostility, and rage

+ personal distress and unrest
+ a sense of loss or of "missing something"
+ helplessness and frustration
+ guilt, inadequacy, sense of failure
+ injustice or "wrongness"
+ tribulation, hardship, and trial
+ discomfort and confusion
+ questioning and doubts
+ philosophical dis-ease
+ psychological angst
+ a spiritual "dark night of the soul"

This new language of grief feelings may be unfamiliar. Or some of these feelings may immediately ring a familiar note in our psyche, as we recognize them from our own life. A man might have an "Aha!" experience as he reads this list: "I've felt that before! I know what that's like!" It is my hope that as men, we can begin to identify with some of these grief feelings and experiences in our own lives. For we need to *name our pains and speak our hurts* before we can find relief and healing. If you have not felt the pangs of grief thus far in your life, thank the good Lord! But rest assured that sooner or later you will.

+ Do any of the descriptions above apply to you?
+ Is there a sense of loss, of pain, or of something missing from your life right now?
+ Where are the griefs of your life right now?

A father faces his grief

Hundreds of doubts assailed me as I struggled to adjust to the reality of my situation and to make some sense out of his death. . . . I could not imagine ever being happy again. I didn't think I would ever enjoy my life. I missed my son terribly, and I was consumed with worry about my family. The question of "why" continued to plague me. I guess I was asking for knowledge and insight which no mortal can have. It was like a midnight search in a dark room for a black cat that wasn't there.

> *When we lose faith in the possibility of ever regaining happiness, we don't allow ourselves to believe that we can hope again. In truth, believing that we will get better IS healing. . . . Start with the fact that you ARE. Try to find some sense of gratitude about your own life. Don't try to figure out the why. . . . You never will.*
>
> Jeff Dyson, Compassionate Friends *newsletter, Spring 1994*

Redefining the limits of grief

As you can see, there are many misconceptions about grief in our world today. We men (and our women friends) reading this book need to realize that *grief is not limited to death and funerals*. Too often when we hear of grief, we instinctively think of funeral parlors, deathbeds, terminal diseases, cemeteries, morbidity, and death in general. Certainly grief includes these crucial situations, but it is far too narrow a perspective to limit our interpretation of grief simply to the end of human life.

This narrow perspective of grief is part of the larger societal problem with men and emotions (as well as with death and grieving). By limiting grief to funerals and dying, society cuts us off from the broad and encompassing spectrum of grief feelings that lie dormant within us. We have a hard enough time as it is dealing with our hidden inner world and feelings. Limiting grief to death and funerals only further entrenches us in our inability to confront all the hurts, losses, and sorrows within us.

The truth of the matter is that *any event in life that involves loss or failure can be a source of grief feelings*. Job loss or transfer, divorce or separation, disease or serious sickness, work struggles or conflicts, financial failures, midlife crisis, vocational uncertainty —all of these are likely sources for the rise of grief feelings.

Sometimes, it's not even a life-threatening or life-changing situation that triggers our griefquest. Some men wake up, look into the mirror, and suddenly realize, "I'm going bald!" or "Summer has ended and winter is around the corner" or "I can't drive to the hoop like I used to five years ago!" And, lo, the hidden realm of grief slowly emerges with its dark shadows and all of its dreary implications.

At a businessman's lunch a man said, "I have spent the last thirty years of my life reaching the top rung of the world's ladder of success. I now feel in my heart I was for all those years on the wrong ladder." Life had passed him by. Sure he had money, but the wealth was acquired at the expense of intimacy with and the affection of his family and friends.
David Smith, The Friendless American Male

The Dennis Byrd story

Dennis Byrd was a six-foot-five, 270-pound defensive tackle in 1989, the year he was drafted as a rookie by the New York Jets football team. He had an outstanding rookie year, ending with seven sacks, one short of the Jets' rookie record, and was named to one All-Rookie Team. He was in his third year of professional football, rapidly gaining a reputation for himself, when the Kansas City Chiefs came to Giants Stadium on 29 November 1992. The second half had just begun when, in attempting to sack the Chief's quarterback, David Kreig, Byrd crashed into a 280-pound teammate, breaking Byrd's neck and causing almost total paralysis.

Over the next six months, he struggled not only with hospitals, specialists, doctors, therapy sessions, and wheelchairs, but also with his own griefquest search for meaning and purpose. Despite his strong and unshakable faith in God, Dennis grappled with the shocking fact that his entire world had suddenly and tragically changed forever. In the powerful book he later wrote called *Rise and Walk,* he expresses poignantly his own sudden, overwhelming griefs:

Tortuous feelings and emotions were flooding through me for a long time. Questions without answers beat through my brain. It's hard to explain how much my physicality meant to me, how much it means to any professional athlete. I had a beautiful wife, a beautiful daughter . . . those things were really important to me, but so was my body. I was fast, I was strong, among the best in the world at the game I loved. My body said, "Hey, look. I'm a professional football player. I do this." Now I wondered how I could validate myself to her [his wife Ange] without being a football hero. I wondered how she'd feel about me if the football player was gone. . . .

I had to have an MRI test . . . a claustrophobic experience for anyone, but in my case, it was terrifying [since] the tubes are built for average-sized human bodies. It was one of the most horrifying experiences of my life. . . . I was so scared . . . five times they had to stop the test and pull me out. Five times the whole cycle of fear and terror began again.

[Then] they were going to put a halo vest on my head, put screws in me. Once more I had to gather the strength to stay calm. They marked four spots, . . . gave me a shot of xylocaine at each of those spots. Then they simply began screwing. I remember the metal pins crunching through my skin. Not squeaking. Crunching. All this pushing and pressure were frightening. . . . Breathing was hard enough already . . . and now I had this vest adding to that feeling of constriction. It was 1:00 a.m. when the procedure was done.

Ange was there as they laid me in bed. I fell asleep haunted by a question that would wake me up in the middle of many nights to come. Was this really happening to me? I knew I would never play football again. That was over. But walking, being well again, and right away. I found myself imagining that somehow . . . I'd wake up after an operation and my limbs would be back. I was hoping for that.

Dennis Byrd did walk again, and continues to today, without a cane, looking no more unnatural in his movement than other former football players. He is a powerful example of the male griefquest. Desolated by unexpected tragedy, he was forced to confront and come to grips with a broken body and shattered career.

Dennis freely acknowledges that his faith in God was an immense reason for his healing: "I had to put my faith in that somehow God would make this a miracle, and that miracle could come in many different ways—not necessarily in me walking again, but in the miracle of making me a complete person in whatever I had, whether I was in a wheelchair or not. It was about healing my heart, because I was totally devastated."

I could easily have been destroyed by what happened. I could easily have been broken, just fallen apart. People ask me if I ever asked "Why me?" during these past months. I think of what Arthur Ashe had to say before he died of AIDS-related pneumonia: "If I say 'Why me?' about this," he said, "then I've got to say 'Why me?' about all the good things that have happened in my life." With so much more life ahead of me, how could I possibly ask "Why me?"

Dennis Byrd, Rise and Walk

Grief is not "efficient"

Griefs, losses, and pains in our lives (like those of Dennis Byrd and thousands of others) will *never* be dealt with as efficiently, painlessly, or "cleanly" as we men would like. Many of us unfortunately treat our bodies and inner spirits as we do our automobiles. When there is a problem with the engine or brakes, for example, we bring the car to a mechanic who we fully expect will professionally replace or tune up whatever is amiss. All is quick, clean, efficient, and (except for the bill!) relatively painless.

We seem to expect that *all* life's problems and pains should be dealt with as efficiently and painlessly as this. We ignore our inner world, our insecurities and fears, or else consciously trample them under by strength of will, in the belief that all feelings and emotions are "useless appendages" in the business of everyday life. Thus, feelings of grief, along with those of compassion, tenderness, sensitivity, and others, are relegated to the "out basket" of life because they refuse to disappear into place as efficiently and neatly as we would like!

At the core, it is our *image of our masculine selves* that may be flawed. We are not mechanical machines operating out of some scientifically predetermined, behavioristic causality. We are not soulless, remote, independent islands. *We are living, breathing, divinely inspired, passionate, struggling, weak but beautiful human beings!* We are an integral combination of physical body, inner spirit and soul, personality, and emotion. We ignore and overlook our hidden inner world, our grief feelings, only at great peril to our psychological balance.

We men must be willing to change our image of ourselves and learn the "dark" and different language of grief. The griefquest we will walk in these pages is primarily a journey into the most mysterious but magnificent frontier in the world—ourselves. Our griefquest will inevitably lead to the doorway of a new land—an uncomfortable, unfamiliar, and dark place perhaps, but a place of new confidence, healthier living, and a new masculine wisdom. For now, every man reading this chapter needs to know this one simple fact: you who have been battered and torn from the jousts and struggles of life *will* find this "brave new world." No quest guided by the Power that created this world ever goes unfulfilled. Dennis Byrd and the thousands of other men who have walked this road before us are living stories of the healing power of griefquest.

People age prematurely because they are unable to embrace new ideas, and because they continue to mistake their own prejudices for the laws of nature.

Ashley Montagu, anthropologist

CHAPTER TWO

Do men grieve differently than women?

Steve's story—Love despite differences

Steve and Sue have been happily married since July 1983. They have four children, have participated in Marriage Encounter weekends, and have worked hard at their relationship. But after more than fifteen years of being together, Steve freely admits that they often wonder how they ever got together in the first place:

> My wife and I are as different as night and day. We often joke about just how radical the differences are between us. We end up concluding that only God, in God's warped sense of humor, could have brought us together and nurtured our relationship over the last twelve years.
>
> We cope with the big hurts in life very differently as well. Yet somehow we accept each other's differences and continue to nudge each other toward wholeness, which is what it's all about anyway. The following chart depicts at a glance the two ends of the coping spectrum that we have typically encountered in our relationship.

Sue	Steve
◆ Freely expresses her feelings	◆ Just feels numb inside
◆ Turns to friends for support	◆ Tries to go it alone
◆ Allows tears to flow freely	◆ Keeps things inside

- ◆ Seeks help from all available sources
- ◆ Doesn't rush the process

- ◆ Feels stigmatized to seek help
- ◆ Seeks information, reads books
- ◆ Wants to get it over with

Steve continues:

The above dynamic reflects our own experience from twelve years of marriage, and it might reflect yours as well. I really don't relish the fact that I sound like such a typical male! I think that I should somehow be more enlightened than that. I hate to admit it, but I admire my wife for her innate coping skills. I try to be in touch with what our society calls the more "feminine" qualities. Suffice it to say, though, that they just don't come very naturally.

When it comes to the question of how and why men and women grieve differently, so much comes down to the "dirty" word *socialization*. Men and women are so different, and in so many ways! I am fascinated by the difference between the sexes. . . . The bestseller list always contains a blockbuster title or two that attempts to sort things out. . . .

Men and women—Vive la différence!

Men and women are different. This basic truth seems self-evident to all, but in today's gender-sensitive world, it is a truth that continues to be analyzed. Sexual and biological differences are fairly obvious, but psychological and behavioral differences are more in dispute.

Couples like Steve and Sue are not unique. Many couples can relate to their divergent coping mechanisms. Men and women often take very different approaches to handling everyday life issues, and crisis and grief are no exceptions. Anyone who has ever been in a close friendship with a member of the opposite sex has probably entertained the thought so well expressed by John Gray's popular book title *Men Are from Mars, Women Are from Venus*.

Certainly men and women do share many common psychological growth patterns. But each sex has its own unique ways of developing those basic behavioral, psychological, and personal traits that make us who we are. This is not the place nor time to enter into arguments surrounding gender-related personality traits. But suffice it to say that it is our belief that men do develop some uniquely masculine aspects of personality (as women do feminine traits).[1]

The masculine aspect of personality may be variously described as logos, or outgoing reason, active creativity, controlled aggressiveness, psychological firmness, the capacity to strive for goals and overcome obstacles en route.

John Sanford, The Kingdom Within

Neither the male aspects and behavioral tendencies nor the female aspects or tendencies[2] are "better" than the other. Both sexes complement each other physically, psychologically, and in many other ways, as God's "natural law" planned it. Jungian psychology has likewise taught us that men have a feminine side to their personality (called *anima*), as women have a masculine side *(animus)*. So, what we describe here are not unchanging dictums about men and women's behavior, but rather *inclinations and tendencies.* These inclinations can help explain behavior patterns at times of grief and loss, but certainly are not proscriptive of *all* male (or female) actions or attitudes.

Having said this, one basic tendency in masculine nature seems to center around men's need for independence and autonomy. Maintaining a certain freedom in action and attitude is very important for many men. (This may well reflect the basic survival needs of our prehistoric male ancestors.) Competitiveness tends to thrive among men; indeed it is the way many men "feel out" their status and rank with their peers. Likewise, men often feel tension between maintaining a social image (being in control) and the inner emotional turmoil that may boil up in crisis. Expressing that inner turmoil, of course, seems to be not only socially unacceptable but a sign of weakness.

All of this differs from women, who tend to be more highly relational than men. Women often have a support network that encourages and promotes sharing on personal and emotional levels. Likewise, women are far more likely to express their emotions and to display empathy and compassion in response to the emotions of others.

Maryland grief counselor Tom Golden sums up some of these differences very accurately when he says: "The key word for women is *intimacy*, which is a measure of the degree that women are related to each other. Men have a key word of *independence*. The object of their striving . . . is to maintain and enhance their independence and position."[3]

Along with these psychological differences, research is emerging that indicates that chemical and hormonal differences may affect the underlying nature of men and women. For example, William Frey, in *Crying: The Mystery of Tears*, theorizes that declining amounts of the hormone prolactin in men after adolescence make it more difficult for them to access tears in times of great emotion.[4] A *Time* magazine article several years ago also reported research showing that differences in the size of a membrane connecting the two hemispheres of the brain might give women a greater connection between verbal capacity and feelings, leaving men less able to verbalize feeling states.[5] *Newsweek* recently covered research being done on differences in how men's and women's brains actually function, using MRI and other brain-mapping technologies.[6]

All of this illustrates the point that men and women can be quite different in how they approach essential life issues. There are substantial psychological, physical, and cultural reasons for this. Thus, it should not come as a surprise that how men deal with grief and loss may also be quite different from women. The generic advice often heard for griefwork ("Let out your feelings. Don't be afraid to cry," and so on) may not work as easily for a man as a woman. A man's griefquest is a unique journey through an often foreign and strange land.

Do not try to make males into female mourners. This is unrealistic. Men may never cry as frequently as women do, but this does not mean they cannot express their sadness in other ways. . . . They do not have to do it the same way as women.

Therese Rando, Grieving: How to Go On
Living When Someone You Love Dies

A couple mourns: Two different grief styles

One of the most difficult griefs to face is the loss of a young child. Apart from the loss itself, a couple faces the strain of an often stressed marital relationship, a changed family structure, as well as the struggle to find a "reason" for an unexplainable event.[7] They also bear the burden of two differing grief styles clashing head-on: the father may mourn in a way inexplicable to his wife, while the mother's style may seem completely foreign and even uncomfortable to her husband.

I have noticed this contrast several times in my ministry as a priest, most recently in 1994. A couple in the church where I was stationed had lost a much beloved eighteen-month-old baby to a sudden viral infection that left him in a weeklong coma. At week's end, the couple finally made the difficult decision to withdraw life support, and shortly afterward the formal medical pronouncement of death was made.

Both, of course, experienced utter shock, disbelief, and the numbness of emotions that naturally accompanies such a sudden and unexpected tragedy. They both experienced disrupted lifestyles, upset patterns for everyday activities, depression, and an immense void in their lives. But there were noticeable differences in their individual grieving patterns.

The father, Tyrone, cried briefly when he and Nakia held their baby just after removing him from life support, but after that I saw no more tears. He appeared stoic and unmoved on the surface by the events swirling around him. Tyrone had a certain ability to "objectify" the situation, to become immensely practical even at the moments of greatest intensity and grief (planning things that needed to be done, for example). The only feelings he was able to speak about and own were those of guilt—for not having "done more," for feeling a sense of relief when the baby finally died after being removed from life support, for buying a newspaper and wanting to read it shortly after the final death pronouncement. Aside from me, I don't think Tyrone talked about himself and his feelings to anyone else. His trust in God, his hope and belief in life and even in healing remained strong and unshakable in his words and actions throughout the entire process.

Tyrone and Nakia's other son, a twelve-year-old junior high student, remained generally unreadable emotionally, showing little response in his feelings or outward expression. But one poignant event betrayed his gender inclination and cultural training. At one point, he held his baby brother in his arms, rather awkwardly and for no more than a minute or so. Then he began crying, immediately wanting to leave and get out of the hospital. He asked if he could call up some friends, and eventually went to spend time with his sixteen-year-old cousin. The turmoil of his inner grief had certainly overwhelmed the youth, and his "maleness" (and young age) prevented any open expression or confronting of those new and foreign inner feelings.

The baby's mother grieved openly and freely, and was deeply and radically torn apart by the loss of her baby. Her faith, personal strength, and family support have helped her make it through this horrible period, but to this day (twelve months later) she remains deeply "in process," working through the feelings and issues the grief has surfaced. Tears flowed freely and often. She verbalized constantly her fears, concerns, and rambling thoughts (often illogical and disconnected but still very real and valid). She connected daily (sometimes hourly!) with friends, family, clergy, all the people in her life who held a special place and could empathize. Nakia's daily routine went into numbing upheaval and confusion as she struggled with depression, grief, and loss.

Both Tyrone and Nakia have dealt with their grief fairly effectively, but in very different ways. Tyrone reacted much in line with the psychological inclinations of most men toward life in general. Nakia dealt with her grief in line with the feminine tendencies mentioned above. We see two differing styles of grieving, with important elements common and essential to both. One style of grieving is not necessarily better than the other—they are in reality *complementary* to each other.

They that love beyond the world cannot be separated by it. Death is but crossing the world, as friends do the seas; they live in one another still.

William Penn

The male grieving pattern

Do men grieve? Yes, they *can* grieve, *do* grieve, and *need* to grieve. Males tend to grieve differently than women, and with greater difficulty and irregularity, given some inherent obstacles in their path. Tyrone's way of dealing with his son's death was reflective of many of the factors mentioned above, as well as perhaps his own ethnic (African American) heritage, and his parenting-husbanding style.

Do men know how to grieve? Do they do it naturally or easily? Generally speaking, no. Many men find it extremely difficult to grieve because of cultural, psychological, and perhaps even physical differences. Carol Staudacher, in her fine work *Men and Grief*, says that "men who do express, release or completely work through their grief are the *exception* rather than the rule." Personally, I neither agree nor disagree with this statement, because I see the truth of both sides of the coin. I know of any number of men who *have* apparently dealt effectively and completely with their grief and loss, but certainly a greater number who are in varying degrees of denial, inner pain, and half-traveled griefquests.

There are a number of features in the male griefquest pattern that tend to set us apart from women. These are not exclusively male, nor definitive of all male grieving but, again, are instinctive *tendencies* in men (factors that certainly can be present in women's grief as well).

First, men are inclined toward private expression of grief, where few emotions are shown publicly, or even admitted personally. In Staudacher's book *Men and Grief*, this is described as "solitary mourning" or "secret grief." Grief is held within, for a variety of reasons—because we are not relational but autonomous by nature, because we do not wish to burden anyone else with these "useless" grief feelings, and because we are simply not comfortable with (or, at times, even aware of) the turmoil and pain hidden inside us.

Like the dark, murky waters of an unchanging forest swamp, private grief feelings that are unexpressed can stagnate within a man. Unprocessed grief can contribute to heart attacks, ulcers, alcoholism, and cancer. Other physical problems can also arise: insomnia, trouble with concentration or clear thinking, fatigue, lack of energy, depression, anger, aggressiveness, or even violence.

The private expression of grief is not necessarily unhealthy for a man. The essential issue here is the acknowledging and honoring of inner grief—however a man does it—not the public or outward expression of grief feelings. Again, male and female grieving styles are *complementary*, not *contradictory*.

Psychotherapist Thomas Golden believes that the key for men expressing grief is knowing that they are respected first.[8] When a man knows that he has the respect of other men, that they will honor his autonomy and accept his "weakness," he will feel free to take the risk of admitting his grief, insecurity, and other fears.

In actual fact, the "I'm all right, I don't need to talk" approach is often not a sign that a man is doing fine but a cover-up for his inability to express painful feelings.
    Christopher Lukas and Henry Seiden, Silent Grief

Second, most grieving men feel it is important to maintain control and their "image." Keeping tight control over his emotional world is an attempt to maintain control of his life and everything that happens to him. Most men have learned growing up that "emotional vulnerability denotes weakness." So, when a man breaks down, revealing his inner uncertainties, he may fear losing his image or status with other men in the competitive game of life. Thus, when grief and loss confront a man, he instinctively tends to deal with this problem as he does with all others—by staying calm, in control, on top of things, showing no weakness.

One man exemplified this inclination to control when he told me: "My wife is too emotional about death. I'm not comfortable with her when she does that. . . . It's a foreign world for me. I've got to keep her going and stay strong, even though I'm hurting like crazy and don't know what to do." This man found his own grief process complicated by his wife's strong emotions, because he felt he had to be the "strong one," thus maintaining his image at a time when his own inner turmoil was crying out for acknowledgment.

Overcontrol of emotions and image is one of the greatest dangers to a successful griefquest. Repressing emotions and preserving one's image solves nothing in itself and leads to the "pressure cooker" principle: what is repressed in one area will surface again in another. The goal of griefquest is healthy detachment from the loss, *not* from the emotions connected to it. Pain must be experienced and honored somehow—by talking, thinking, crying, writing, daring, confronting. We'll speak more on this in the second half of this book.

It's not easy to be a man. If I express my grief I lose, because I violate the male stereotype of the strong man who shows no emotions. However, I know if I don't express the pain of grief, I will also lose because suppressing my feelings will bring me more problems. I'm in a no-win situation.

Frank (a widower after thirty-eight years of marriage)

Last, men have a tendency toward action and activity at times of grief. Men value independence in thought and action but are not always as good at handling inner emotions. Thus, at times of grief, men tend to utilize their strength—namely, taking concrete action and "doing things" (described by John Sanford as "outgoing reason, active creativity" in *The Kingdom Within*). Because grief feelings cannot be handled cleanly and efficiently, and are often immensely frustrating for men (who can't really "do" anything about them), men seem to need to grab hold of something that can be actively and efficiently done. Thus, they can bring control to an intrinsically out-of-control situation and feel that they are accomplishing something constructive and healthy.

Some men become almost obsessive with activity, however, finding things to occupy every waking moment—errands, work, activities around the house, even legal actions or compulsive physical exercise. Although some therapists feel that men *need* to return to work soon after a death or great loss, an obsession with staying busy can become simply a method to avoid or bury inner pain. When a man gets so immersed in activity, there is no time for grief, painful inner feelings, or even thinking about loss. A little activity to process grief or channel pent-up energy is one thing, but massive, persistent activity to avoid grief is unhealthy.

Activity can become a tremendous source of healing for men on their griefquest. In choosing appropriate actions (creative actions), a man can enter into his grief and begin to process the pain and acknowledge its role in his life. Using this innate inclination toward activity can also become a way for men to honor their griefquest in unique, memorializing ways. (One man, for example, chopped and stacked wood to help vent his grief energy; another man found that painting was the most therapeutic thing he could do.) This concept of creative activity is such a vitally important one for men that we will devote a full chapter to it later on in the book.

In summary, the differences between men and women are also apparent in how they handle grief. Though men generally do not grieve easily nor smoothly, still we must learn to express and honor our grief, using uniquely masculine patterns, or else unhealthy consequences can result. In learning to walk a griefquest, the first step is becoming aware of the obstacles and cultural barriers we men have unconsciously grown up with and accepted. That is the next step we will take in our search for healthy male grieving.

In December 1987, actor Ben Vereen received news that his sixteen-year-old daughter had been killed in an auto accident. "It was like someone had reached in and just ripped my heart out," Vereen recalls. He turned to alcohol and drugs. "I plunged into self-destruction physically, mentally, and spiritually. I just went on a death spiral and didn't care to get out of it." Vereen's griefquest only ended when he moved out of his private depression and "reconnected with my spirituality." Upon releasing control to a greater Power, he found peace in a Reality bigger than himself.
    Victor Parachin, "Grief Relief: Helping Men Mourn,"
    Catholic Cemetery, November 1995

Notes

1. Richard Rohr identifies the characteristics of uniquely "masculine energy" very effectively in his tape series *A Man's Approach to God*, tape 2. John Sanford (a Jungian psychotherapist and writer) also discusses this point in a number of his books.

2. John Sanford describes the feminine aspect of personality as "eros, or the capacity for relationships, understanding, awareness of others, creativity through receptiveness, an indirect way of attaining goals, patience, compassion, the valuation and nourishing of life." He then cautions, "everyone contains possibilities for both masculine and feminine development, and no one can approach wholeness without development in both areas." Cf. *The Kingdom Within* (Mahwah, NJ: Paulist Press, 1970), pp. 33–34.

3. Thomas Golden, *Gender and Cultural Differences in Grief*, 10400 Connecticut Avenue, Suite 514, Kensington, MD, 20895.

4. William Frey, *Crying: The Mystery of Tears* (Minneapolis: Winston Press, 1985). In the 1976 book *Grief in Cross-Cultural Perspectives*, Rosenblatt, Walsh, and Jackson examined the grieving of eighty-seven

different cultures. They did not find one culture in which men expressed more tears than women and found nine cultures in which men did not cry at all. This highlights another distinction between men and women, namely that men do not use tears as much as women when dealing with their grief.

5. Christine Gorman, "Sizing Up the Sexes," *Time*, January 20, 1992, pp. 42–51.

6. Sharon Begley, "Gray Matters," *Newsweek*, March 27, 1995, pp. 48–54.

7. Buz Overbeck, who works with a group called Grief Resource Foundation in Dallas, Texas, has developed material for how couples respond to the loss of a child. In a seminar he does called "She Cries . . . He Sighs," he talks about the five facts of parents' grief: (1) The intensity of *his* grief is dependent on his pre-death relationship with the fetus, baby, or child. (2) The intensity of *her* grief is dependent on the place the pregnancy or child held in her hopes, dreams, future, self-esteem, and self-worth. (3) Most fathers resolve (or make peace) with their grief in 3–6 months. (4) Most mothers need 9–24 months to resolve their grief. (5) Most men feel their spouses need professional help after 3–6 months.

8. Thomas Golden, op. cit., p. 10.

CHAPTER THREE

Why do men ignore not only grief but feelings in general?

John's story—His father's son

John is a big, strong man, a former athlete, who has worked hard on personal growth. After his wife nearly left him, he understood that he needed to work more on his marriage relationship. In doing so, he realized how much a product of his upbringing he was, and especially how his father's attitudes and actions influenced him. He shares his thoughts here:

> I have realized that I am my father's son. For as long as I can remember, I've called him "strong like bull." He's a big man and can be described as the stereotypical strong, silent type. I can recall the times he has cried on one hand—the death of my grandmother, my mom's severe aneurysm, and his extreme frustration at having to care for my mom—the latter shared when we were both pretty well lubricated after several drinks!
>
> I have seen how his coping style (or lack thereof) has negatively affected his well-being, both physically and emotionally. I've tried to encourage him to get help but he has stubbornly refused. . . . He's had episodes of severe angina and a couple of heart attacks that seem to me obviously related to his heavy heart. He lacks a sense of empowerment to change his situation and is generally pessimistic about the future.

I have learned much about myself by observing my dad's behavior. Maybe I even now define myself in *opposition* to certain negative aspects of it. I guess I've realized deep down that the cycle of dysfunction does not need to be perpetuated.

Even though I am my father's son and proud of it, I do not necessarily need to manifest those negative behaviors that are destructive and unhealthy just because we are part of the same gene pool.

I have begun to explore my inner world and have learned new coping styles with myself and my wife . . . styles that promote emotional health and well-being. I have experienced generational healing and discovered a newfound freedom from paternal entanglements. At the same time, however, compassion for my father and his woundedness continues to deepen.

Lack of trust in other men, guardedness of feelings, remoteness . . . it is likely that you received these messages from your father, and now see them in yourself. Not only did you learn these "typical" male behaviors from your father, but for the last several generations, they have been supported by the culture throughout the industrial age.

Steven Farmer, The Wounded Male

The restraints of being born a man

For me personally, it is very ironic to hear the criticisms of masculinity that have become so commonplace in today's world. Men are criticized for their traditional domination of the business world, the workplace, the church, politics, marriage roles, and many other areas of life (not without some justification, I might add). Male "insensitivities" are constantly berated and joked about. Our supposed lack of feelings is an unending source of complaint. Our "warlike" aggressiveness and assertiveness are blamed for nearly every societal ill. Our inadequacies and struggles in personal relationships are daily conversation topics for frustrated women and friends. It has perhaps never been so unpopular to be a man in America!

And yet the great irony is that men have perhaps never been so misunderstood! Never have men been so poised to break through to new, deeper levels of male consciousness, insight, and sensitivity. Never have men been so willing to re-examine our roles in society, to change traditional male-female stereotypes and personal behavior patterns. Never have we been more conscious of how *hard* it is to be a man in the world—of all the restraints, pressures, burdens, and restrictions (from within and without) placed upon us as we are born and raised in twentieth-century American society.

There are a number of reasons why men, in many ways, have the deck stacked against them. While admitting that we men have much in our behavior patterns that needs to be confronted and changed, still certain pressures and limitations we grow up with are enormous barriers to developing healthy, emotionally comfortable, positive personalities. Our unhealthy dealing with grief and loss is but one casualty of a generally dysfunctional male upbringing that discourages men from tending to their inner lives in any way.

Given society's strictures on men, it is remarkable that any man expresses the pain of grief and works through a loss until it is resolved. Male sex role conditioning acts strongly, and in direct opposition to the requirements necessary to grieve a loss.

Carol Staudacher, Men and Grief

Allow me to outline some of the pressures men grow up with and to elaborate upon them briefly:

1. Men lack strong role models in their formative years.
Every child grows and learns by example. When young boys grow

up with absent fathers, in single female–parent homes, or with men unable or unwilling to model deeper, more sensitive ways of being "a man," the behavior patterns for those boys' entire future begin to be formed. Men cannot easily learn on their own how to be comfortable expressing emotions, or to develop an inner life of integrity and awareness, or to warmly and openly embrace their wife, or to verbally express their love of God. These are all ac-tions reflective of a "true man," but *not* taught or affirmed by our modern culture. These attitudes are best *caught*, not *taught*. Too many of us have never had gentle-men to "catch" them from.

Ten Commandments of the Traditional Male

1. *Thou shalt not cry or expose other feelings of emotion, fear, weakness, sympathy, empathy, or involvement before thy neighbor.*
2. *Thou shalt not be vulnerable, but honor and respect the "log-ical," "practical," or "intellectual"—as thou defines them.*
3. *Thou shalt not listen except to find fault.*
4. *Thou shalt condescend to women in the smallest and biggest of ways.*
5. *Thou shalt control thy wife's body.*
6. *Thou shalt have no other egos before thee.*
7. *Thou shalt have no other breadwinners before thee.*
8. *Thou shalt not be responsible for housework before anybody.*
9. *Thou shalt honor and obey the straight-and-narrow pathway to success: job specialization.*
10. *Thou shalt have an answer to all problems at all times.*

Warren Farrell, The Liberated Man

2. Society doesn't permit men to be emotionally free. The public mores of our modern culture are strict in what they "allow" a man to act like in public. Attitudes like these abound: "Men must always be strong for their family." "Men must remain in con-trol at all times, must never shed a tear or show emotion pub-licly." "The effective, successful man is one who at all times is cool, unemotional, detached, businesslike." Like Maine Senator Edmund Muskie in the 1972 presidential race, who shed tears publicly, when men do dare to break society's taboos, it is considered a sign of weakness and failure. The consequences of this can be severe, as they were for Senator Muskie, who soon after withdrew from the race.

Resolved at an early age to be a soldier-officer like the greatwarriors of his ancestors, [George] Patton . . . all his life honed his image, developing what he felt were the appropriate mannerisms—profanity in language, aristocratic bearing, the fierce scowl, ruthlessness. And in the process he killed much of his sensitivity and warmth and thereby turned a sweet-tempered and affectionate child into a seemingly hard-eyed and choleric adult.

Martin Blumenson, Patton: Man Behind the Legend

---

3. Most men lack true deep friendships. While men may have many drinking buddies, or watch sports together with their regular gang, many men don't have even one truly close male friend. Men seem to find it hard to accept that they even need friendship with other men. Our inherent competitiveness, aversion to emotions and "weakness," and our independence all combine to make the deep sharing of friendship with another man very difficult.

David Smith says it well in *The Friendless American Male*: "Men must manufacture nonemotional reasons for being together—a business deal must be discussed or a game must be played. Rarely do men plan a meeting together simply because they have a need to enjoy each other's company."[1] Little wonder then that when a man has to face grief, loss, or personal tragedy, he is so unable to ask for help from his brothers.

4. Most men are strangers to their own inner world. Like most women, the majority of men today seem to live shallow, superficial lives. Not only do we go through life avoiding the deeper questions of ultimate meaning and value, but most of us find even looking within ourselves in the smallest way uncomfortable and upsetting. Patrick Arnold, in his fine book *Wildmen, Warriors and Kings*, says that men today live in "the Numbness—an inability to feel joy or meaning or sadness about *anything*. . . . Modernity has created generations of Numb Men who cannot even feel their own experiences, much less articulate them."[2]

Take away money, sex, and power, and most men on this earth do not know how to motivate themselves. They don't know how to make decisions about what they want to do with life, where they want to go, who they want to be. . . . Most Western men don't know how to draw their life from within. Spirituality is precisely a source of energy from within, called spirit, which is beyond money, sex, and power.

Richard Rohr, A Man's Approach to God

---

5. Many men lack a strong spiritual foundation, or a "life of the soul." Too many men grow up with few, if any, positive spiritual experiences of God in their life. Indeed, much of society seems to think that spirituality, or a life of the soul, is a sign of weakness for a man. As a result, many men today are experiencing "spiritual bankruptcy"—a sense of emptiness and disconnectedness in the universe. They have nothing to ground them or give them a sense of purpose or direction in the world. Their "bank account" of moral strength, ethical values, and healthy virtue is bankrupt and empty.

As Arnold says, for many men "spirituality, prayer, and worship belong somehow to the world of women; stained glass windows, elaborate rituals, lacy weddings, and dainty sermons" make men uncomfortable.[3] The absence of God in a man's life denies him one of the most healthy, transforming, and redeeming images of masculinity in this world—namely, that of a God who has taken masculine form, literally becoming a man to bring salvation and hope.

*So Real Men not only eschew quiche, they avoid church too. And
the only times a Real Man goes to church are at his baptism, wedding, or funeral: the "carried, married, and buried" syndrome.*
            Patrick Arnold, Wildmen, Warriors and Kings

**6. Until now, much of the information about grief and loss
was not designed for men.** In researching this book, we discovered how much women writers and women's perspectives have
dominated the area of grief, bereavement, and personal loss. Indeed, the majority of people visiting therapists or overtly attempting to deal with grief issues are women. Thus, it is only natural
that women's perspectives, feelings, and unique concerns have
come to dominate the magazines, books, and therapy styles preva-
lent today in the areas of grief and loss.

Psychotherapist Tom Golden comments specifically on this
in his booklet *A Man's Grief:* "It took me some time to realize
that the type of therapy I had been taught to do was designed for
women. Somehow men didn't seem to fit our program. I began to
realize that there wasn't something wrong with the men—there
was something wrong with the therapy. . . . I have found that
men need grief defined in a different manner."[4]

Until now, men have rarely had literature or therapy specially designed for them in areas like grief and loss. (In fact, the best
book on male grief available at the writing of this book is an excellent one entitled *Men and Grief,* but it is written by a woman,
Carol Staudacher.) Until recently, men have been forced to use
women's models and paradigms for dealing with grief. Certainly
these are helpful and healing, but they often miss the mark in getting to the heart of uniquely male grieving issues.[5]

**7. Inner-city life shows a growing contempt and disregard
for human life.** In our inner cities today, men are killing men with
absolutely no remorse or guilt. For so many young men today, the
tragic truth they have grown up with is "Life is short, and I'll die
early anyway. Who cares?" No man has ever communicated to

these young men their inherent goodness. No man has been there to model healthy, positive ways of dealing with life's problems. As a result, these young men's uniquely male generative gift and power of life is spiritually and psychologically bankrupt, and is reduced (for many) to mere physical "coupling" out of desperation. This utter disregard for life in its fullness is "impotence" in the truest meaning of that term.

I had a feeling I needed help. I was very much a loner. Not because I wanted to be, but because there was nobody around who spoke my language. I kept it all to myself.

A seventy-two-year-old engineer,
as quoted by Carol Staudacher, Men and Grief

In summary

Certainly we men have many factors stacked against us in our attempts to break through to new levels of awareness, sensitivity, and growth. Yet one of the greatest gifts of masculinity has been our traditional strength, courage, and aggressiveness in confronting life's challenges. Whether those challenges have meant hunting for game for a family centuries ago, or finding work to put bread on the table in the modern era—the challenge of the hunt has defined men for generations. Those challenges have brought out the best of men's strengths, gifts, and abilities in every age.

Today, many of the traditional survival challenges men have faced in the past—securing food, safety, shelter, and so on—have disappeared. But men of the present generation find their challenge in a different kind of "hunt." We have confronted and conquered the unknown outer world; now we are faced with the daunting challenge of exploring our inner world. This foreign inner world of powerful emotions is the landscape for a man's griefquest. This inner world of alien feelings and strange "weaknesses" is the unknown frontier for men today. Since few go willingly into new frontiers, grief and loss are one of the few experiences that can forcibly bring men to the brink of this new territory.

By our nature, we men need difficult and daunting challenges to help us grow. We often focus only on the negative aspects of grief and loss, but for men these can be powerful transforming factors both personally and spiritually. They can be *metanoia*,[6] "necessary woundings" that, after sending us through the quicksand of uncertainty, can also break us through to new levels of peace, mental health, success, and personal growth. In other words, we need those times of loss and turmoil for our healthy development.

We would like to elaborate more on this concept of necessary wounding and how grief and loss can be psychologically and spiritually beneficial. In order to do that, we will reflect in the next chapter on men's psychological development.

My father was a good man, and I know now that I was lucky to have a hardworking, concerned father. But I regret that he could never seem to tell me that he loved me. I never felt I learned from him how to act as a man in today's world. I had to learn it on my own. When I asked him once, "Why don't men hug each other?" all he could say was, "Men just don't do things like that! That's for women!"

An anonymous male

Notes

1. David Smith, *The Friendless American Male* (Ventura, CA: Regal Books, 1983), p. 15.

2. Patrick Arnold, *Wildmen, Warriors and Kings* (New York: Crossroad, 1991), pp. 13–14.

3. Ibid., p. 12

4. Thomas Golden, *A Man's Grief*, 10400 Connecticut Avenue, Suite 514, Kensington, MD, 20895, p. 1.

5. For example, dealing with grief purely in terms of feelings and relationships will often be ineffective for a man. These are certainly central issues, but men need to deal with grief and loss more in terms of issues like (1) physical or cognitive body "changes" (which force them to face pain); (2) confronting traditional male stereotypes of independence and unwillingness to "burden" anyone with their pains (which are "signs of weakness"); (3) finding activities or "ritual actions" that will enable them to get in touch with their inner grief or pain.

6. *Metanoia* is a Greek word and biblical term meaning repentance or "change of heart." It implies an attitude of turning oneself around or turning back to God after having sinned or fallen short of the mark.

CHAPTER FOUR

Can grief and loss be important in men's development?

This chapter attempts to put grief and loss into a larger life perspective for men. Because we touch on some of the psychological, philosophical, and developmental principles that underlie masculinity, this chapter is a little "heavier" than the others. Some may find it helpful in deepening their perspective on the masculine grief process; some may not. Feel free to skip lightly over some of this if you're not at a place in life where you feel it's important for you. In other words, we give you permission not to read this chapter! (That's for all Catholics and others reared with compulsive, perfectionistic tendencies!)

Tommy Dorsey—How grief changed a life

Originally from Georgia, Tommy Dorsey came to Chicago in 1919 to pursue a jazz and blues career. After achieving fame as a jazz musician, Dorsey joined Pilgrim Baptist Church on Chicago's south side, and became interested in writing his own brand of music, combining jazz and blues with church music. By the early 1930s, he had a large following and was in some demand as a guest musician.

In August 1932, Tommy was asked to be a soloist in Saint Louis for religious services there. His wife was pregnant with their first child. Despite reservations, Dorsey went to Saint Louis to perform. While performing, a messenger gave him a devastating telegram: "Your wife just died." Dorsey later said he was struck by the irony of people happily singing and shouting around him, while he was hardly able to keep from crying out. On arriving back in Chicago, it was confirmed that his wife had died, but had given birth just prior to her death. "I swung between grief and joy," Dorsey recalled. Later that night the baby, too, died. Both his wife and the baby were buried in the same casket.

"I fell apart," he later said. "For days I closeted myself. I felt that God had done me an injustice. I didn't want to serve him anymore. I just wanted to go back to the jazz world I once knew so well." A friend helped the grieving musician then, unwittingly leading to a new era in Dorsey's life. "I sat down at the piano [he led me to], my hand began to browse over the keys. Something happened to me then. I felt as though I could reach out and touch God. I found myself playing a melody, one I'd never heard or played before, and the words came into my head:

> Precious Lord, take my hand, lead me on, let me stand,
> I am tired, I am weak, I am worn,
> Through the storm, through the night, lead me on to the
> light,
> Take my hand, precious Lord, lead me home.

Dorsey added that "as God gave me these words and melody, he also healed my spirit. I learned when I was in the deepest grief, when I felt the farthest from God, that was when he was closest, and when I was the most open to change and healing." Dorsey's life was altered forever by the grief of losing his wife and child, but his wounds led to the composing of more than four hundred other gospel songs, which have touched and inspired millions of people.

There are no great men, only great challenges ordinary men are called to meet.

Admiral William "Bull" Halsey

Life is difficult

Few men ever consciously choose to go through personal trauma, loss, or grief. Death, job loss, depression, midlife crisis—all of these cross the path of every man unexpectedly, without warning or preparation. Thus, grief and pain are a fact of life. M. Scott Peck says it well in the opening words of *The Road Less Traveled:* "Life is difficult." Though we struggle constantly to find a peaceful, stressfree place in the universe, grief, loss, and pain happen.

It is *how men react to these crises* that sets us apart from one another. Some men choose complete denial of their pain and hurt. Some men choose to repress and push back the onslaught of uncertain and confusing feelings that threaten to overwhelm them. Some men choose merely to cope, to adjust their immediate circumstances as needed, avoiding deeper nagging issues and questions. Some men allow their losses and griefs to lead them into something deeper, something transforming, something that opens new vistas and levels in the depths of their being.

These last men, perhaps a minority, are our true masculine heroes: they have faced the harshest challenges of life, learning new and often painful wisdom from them. Ultimately, they emerged from their griefquest with renewed self-knowledge and divinely motivated humbleness, committed to the productive passing on of what they learned during their time of trial.

> *We shall not cease from exploration . . . and the end of all our exploration will be to arrive where we started and know the place for the first time.*
>
> T. S. Eliot, Four Quartets

A look at male development

As a delicious Macintosh apple does not ripen overnight, so too the healthy, mature man does not spring automatically into being

after adolescence. A man's development process requires many seasons, stages, transformations, and defining moments. Every man is
unique, and every life is a singular, rare experience. In the rapidly
growing literary field of men's growth issues, a number of writers
have offered very insightful patterns of male psychological development. Daniel Levinson (*Seasons of a Man's Life*), John Robertson (*Death of a Hero, Birth of the Soul*), and Carl Jung are examples
of men who have outlined helpful stages or metaphors for men's
developmental process.[1]

The following pattern for masculine individuation or development is general enough to cover most common male growth
patterns, yet fluid enough to allow for individual experience. Some
men seem to be more self-aware and interested in personal growth
than others and would thus be more "enlightened" and concerned
about these stages. Other men are less conscious of inner growth
stages and don't seem to care in the least about psychological or
spiritual growth. A man's consciousness of these stages is essentially irrelevant, at least in regard to their presence and effect. The
reality of *some* movement through stages of growth in life is a fact.
Awareness of this movement can benefit a man greatly in dealing
with grief, loss, or any significant struggle in life.[2]

The Four Ages of Man

He with body waged a fight,
But body won; it walks upright.
Then he struggled with the heart;
Innocence and peace depart.
Then he struggled with the mind;
His proud heart he left behind.
Now his wars on God begin;
At stroke of midnight God shall win.

William Butler Yeats

---

1. The unconscious perfection of childhood. This first
stage in a man's growth encompasses the early years of his life,

characterized by youthful ideals of beauty, faith, and trust. This is almost a "Garden of Eden" time—a time of living under unconscious illusions, when we tend to be naive and boastful, and to feel immune from problems, death, and so on. In essence, it is a blissfully unreal and quixotic world. No young man has the slightest thought that death or failure could actually happen to him. Even when negative events occur in his life (and wounds that will affect him permanently), still there remains a deep subconscious illusion of ultimate success and almost grandiose achievement (becoming a basketball superstar, a famous doctor, lawyer, or whatever). This is a time of "inflating one's consciousness," where all things are under our control and everything is possible. There are few boundaries or limits to our ego, psyche, or dreams.

During this essential time of a life, ideals need to be formed, dreams and visions need to flourish freely. These ideals and dreams, as well as healthy childhood parenting and values, will become the foundations of later life for a healthy and balanced masculine identity. The Old Testament prophet Joel wisely says, "Your sons and your daughters shall prophesy . . . , and your young men shall see visions." (Joel 2:28).

There was, in the beginning, a natural self, a magic child, born already full of his own spontaneous energies, interests, talents, appetites, and natural order. How did you feel special as a child? . . . Everything is new, and a boy is open, innocent, trusting, full of wonder and awe. Can you remember this time?

[In this stage of a man's life] the outer world of adventure, conquest, and determination takes total precedence, and a young man strives with relentless energy to build an adult life. He can withstand almost anything in these years with this amazing masculine energy.

Robinson, Death of a Hero, Birth of the Soul

It is a discouraging omen for the future that in today's world many young men seem to be skipping this first stage entirely.

Young men are growing up cold and hardened and becoming streetwise (including gang involvement, drugs, promiscuous sexual activity) because of poverty or circumstances, "father-wounds,"[3] or simple lack of opportunities. This is bound to have (indeed, is *already having*) serious implications for the future not only of our society but also of family life, interpersonal relationships, and the wider workplace environment.

This first stage of "unconscious perfection" and idealism may continue well into adulthood and middle age, in which case (if a man continues in this stage) serious ego problems may develop out of his childish narrow-mindedness and unreality. But at some point in life, most men begin to become aware that all is not as peaceful or problem-free as we have thought. Sometimes (as we will discuss shortly) a crisis or death experience forces a man out of this unreal stage into the next stage of consciousness. However it may happen, a man needs to experience a sense of alienation, suffering, or "complicatedness" that will usher him into the deeper consciousness marking the crucial second stage of growth.

2. The conscious imperfection of the middle years. During this second necessary stage of male development, men slowly begin to become aware of the dualistic nature of life: good is often hopelessly intertwined with evil, and youthful idealistic goals and dreams slowly begin to shatter in the harsh glare of reality. We realize that life is *not* perfect, nor are most relationships, jobs, or people. Suddenly we seem to be surrounded by the complexities of life. Nagging inner questions (or old wounds) rise up, demanding to be heard. Old stabilities such as job and marriage may seem confining and barren as inner uncertainties push up against the now too-comfortable patterns we have established in our life.

For a young person it is almost a sin, at least a danger, to be too preoccupied with oneself; but for the aging person it is a duty and a necessity to devote serious attention to oneself.
Carl Jung, "The Stages of Life,"
Modern Man in Search of a Soul

We have accomplished the first-stage task of developing a strong separate ego. But the universal male psyche falls inevitably into what could be called the "worship of one's accomplishments," which, in turn, creates hubris, narcissism, and a "Type A" machine-like man. A certain falseness (an "out-of-touchness" with their own being) subtly enters into men, and often an imbalanced life-style, an inflated view of oneself, and a lack of perspective and values.

This explains why many men have midlife crises in their late thirties and forties. Though sometimes used to justify selfish, self-promoting activities, for a sincere and honest man, the crisis of this second stage (whether "midlife" or not) can be a profoundly deep, life-changing experience. A deeper inner consciousness begins to emerge, with a nagging call for self-honesty, more "eternal" values, and faithfulness to one's own vision of life and truth.

At this point a man *hopefully* begins to realize he has been living in illusion, in a state of inflation that has been called "infantile grandiosity." Illusions of constant upward progress in the workplace or in spirituality, unending financial success and security, a mate or companion perfect in beauty and personality—the misconceptions in all of these must now be confronted honestly. He must become more grounded in down-to-earth, practical reality.

In traditional spiritual terms, he must learn humility, which literally means "grounded" in truth, knowing the truth about oneself (the Latin root is *humus*, or "earth"). Until a man's often massive pride and inflated ego becomes deflated, or grounded, he will never arrive at true self-awareness, balance, or peace.

It demands a terrible letting-go on the part of the ego to surrender to the Self, which is finally, the Self-for-God. . . . Generally this only happens when the person is driven by pain and frustration to exclaim in words or in the whole of one's being: "I can't do it!"
L. Patrick Carrol and Katherine Dyckman, Chaos or Creation

Unfortunately for men entering this second stage, there is only one way that all of this can occur—through grief and suffering. The movement within requires what Robert Bly in *Iron John* says so well: "the fall, the whirlpool, the sinking through the floor, the Drop, what the ancient Greeks called *katabasis*." Men will resist the deflation of their illusions or being grounded in a deeper consciousness with every fiber of their beings. Perhaps even the majority of them will continue to live "unexamined lives," never taking the time or energy to wrestle with the "wounds that heal." No human being (men especially) wants to change or yield the status quo. Hence, the path to wholeness, peace, and true spirituality (not just "religion") always leads through pain, loss, and grief. The "flying boy" of endless illusions must be grounded.

If a man does not face the pain of things, what Virgil calls the "lacrimae rerum," he will remain forever what John Lee calls a "flying boy." Left to himself, he is dangerous. He is unreal. He certainly won't touch anybody at any significant level. The young man must be taught to weep.

Richard Rohr, Quest for the Grail

By age forty or so, a man has journeyed much in life. Hopefully he has touched "perfection" in some small way (though unaware of it) in his earliest years—with strong foundations of hopefulness, vision, confident action, faith and spirituality, trust in his fellow humans. He has struggled mightily through his middle years to reconcile outer life disappointments and griefs with long-forgotten but undeniable inner truths and wisdom. Now he is able to move toward the third and final stage of masculine development.

3. The conscious perfection of old age. In this final stage of life, a man finally achieves a measure of enlightenment and harmony between his inner and outer worlds. This harmony is perhaps not something that he can actively strive for, but rather something that emerges slowly but surely from years of faithful work, self-reflection, spirituality, and integrity in living. Wise men experience a sense of wholeness in which opposites and tensions are held in rhythmic balance rather than wrestled with or fought against. Wise men have "seen it all," been through personal pain and grief, and have finally uncovered the things of true value and worth in life, the "pearl of great price."

Battles with the ego are for the most part over. A man's ego now falls into its rightful place—not dominating and intimidating (the marks of false masculinity), not passive and "wimpy" (marks of the overly feminine), but reflecting, directing, and focusing his energies into creative action. Men in this stage remain very active, curious, creative, and involved with life. They often have numerous hobbies, projects, interests, and friends. The wise man of this final stage (a *senex*, in Jungian terms) has fought his wars, suffered his wounds, and now has negotiated a gentle peace with the world and God. He does not, as one poet says, "rage against the coming night"; rather, imperfections in people, flaws in the world, problems of aging, even death itself can be calmly accepted. The final "stage" of all life, impending death becomes not an enemy to be feared but a friend to be welcomed.

Perhaps this stage is best understood by meeting a man who is there. A wise, elderly man, wizened by the storms, struggles, and emotions he has passed through, at peace with himself and his God, still interested and active in the larger world about him. This is the "expert" who teaches us by example of this final stage. I hope all of you reading this book have the opportunity to meet such a man. I [Bob] have—you'll read his story in the second half of this book. Louie Miller was for me a companion, brother priest, wise man, grandfather figure, cousin, and friend. Like the true wise man of this final stage, he rarely ever gave me answers, but he helped me ask the right questions. His energy, wisdom, and support have been a guiding light through these three stages of my life. May you be blessed with such a wise man as you walk through your own griefs and losses!

As I get older, I become more aware of the disparity between what I was suited to do with my life, and what I thought I was suited to do. . . . What if I had chosen to become a professor, a communications expert when radio was emerging from its infancy, or a true writer? But then I realize that in the end my life settled into the groove where it best fit. My modest gift is to help people feel a little more comfortable in the frustrations of life. As a priest I've had many opportunities to do that.

Louis G. Miller (unpublished journal entry from 1991)

Grief and loss—The "necessary wounds" that heal

From these stages in men's development, one thing becomes clear immediately. No man moves easily or smoothly from one stage to another. As we've just seen, the normative way that men move forward in self-awareness, faith, and individuation is through pain, deflation, struggle, and loss. In other words, grief (as earlier defined to include any crucial event involving loss or failure) can become a decisive life-changing occurrence for a man. Grief and loss can become a "necessary wound" that energizes and challenges a man to break through to new levels in his consciousness.

Simply put, a necessary wound means that it is the *wound itself that heals*. Though no one in his right mind chooses grief, tragedy, pain, or loss, the irony of our human situation (and the divine wisdom behind it) is that the very things that hurt us the most can transform us, heal us, and renew us! The wounding we receive through our griefs (depression, anger, loneliness, fear, helplessness, or whatever) is *necessary* for growth, new perspectives, personal transformation, and deepened spirituality.

The great psychotherapist Carl Jung discovered this wisdom early in his personal life and in therapy with other people. In his writing and work, he recognized that necessary wounding was required to break free from unconscious ego inflation and blindness.

Jung believed that for men to get in touch with the Self within (that entire deeper, broader inner world), a near inner *revolution* was needed. Namely, everything one had depended on in life might need to seem to be falling apart. Jung affirms that it is only with great pain, disorientation, and tension that a man moves from the outer ego-inflated world to the self-directed inner world.

When we must deal with problems, we instinctively refuse to try the way that leads through darkness and obscurity. We wish only to hear of unequivocal results, and completely forget that these results can only be brought about when we have ventured into and emerged again from the darkness.

Carl Jung, *"The Stages of Life,"*
Modern Man in Search of a Soul

In the vast storehouse of human literature, many examples abound of symbolic wounds that heal, of darkness leading to light. These necessary wounds are the stimuli and motivation not only for great heroic actions but also for inner freedom and healing:

◆ In the myth of Parsifal's search for the Holy Grail, one immediately encounters the wounded Fisher King. His incurable wound leads directly to the long search for the Grail, which ultimately brings healing to the king and the equally wounded land.[4]

◆ In Greek mythology, the centaur Chiron was a skilled healer. However, he was wounded by one of Hercules's poisoned arrows. His injury was incurable; the only relief would be death, but he was not allowed to die. A solution came through the problems of Prometheus, the Titan punished by Zeus for stealing fire and giving it to human beings. Chiron volunteered to go to Hades in Prometheus's place. In this way, Chiron was allowed to die, and Prometheus permitted to go free. Later Chiron was taken from Hades and made an immortal, a fitting reward for his long-suffering and compassion.

The "Chironian wound" was necessary for his destiny. His long-term dealing with that wound earned him immortality. Chiron would never have achieved such a status were it not for the painful wound he endured for so many years.

◆ In our contemporary times, the popular Star Wars movies introduced us to Luke Skywalker, the unknowing son of the evil Darth Vader. In the second movie, Skywalker loses his hand in a lightsaber duel with Vader. This becomes a necessary wound paralleling his father's and helps to teach him the true and proper use of the "Force." Humbled but wiser, Luke not only defeats the evil emperor but wins his father back over to the good side of the Force.

The spirituality of Jesus Christ and Christianity is one of the most powerful sources of wisdom surrounding the necessary wound. Jesus Christ (a brother male, which is a significant coincidence for men) willingly gave his life on the cross. As Isaiah 53:5 says, "he was wounded for our transgressions, / crushed for our iniquities." This action opened up the gates of heaven, the "waters of life," for all those who believe. Thus, 1 Peter 2:24 can say accurately, "by his wounds you have been healed." Jesus' entire life, indeed his very purpose for coming to earth, was to bring healing, Good News, and hope to this world.[5] He ended up accomplishing this not by great miracles or fantastic healings, but only through the wounds of death on a cross.[6]

Father, how wonderful your care for us! To ransom a slave you gave away your Son. O happy fault [felix culpa], O necessary sin of Adam, which gained for us so great a Redeemer!
        From the Exultet *of the Easter Vigil service*

Perhaps Jesus was inspired by the Old Testament story of Jacob wrestling with an angel in Genesis, chapter 32. After an all-night wrestling match, the angel struck Jacob's hip, dislocating it. Jacob would not let the angel leave, however, until he had been granted a blessing. He was given one in the form of the new name *Israel* (wrestler with God), "for you have striven with God," as the angel put it. We are then told that Jacob commented, "I have seen God face to face, and yet my life is preserved." Jacob's injured hip represented a "divine wound," carried forever as a result of his all-night wrestling with God's messenger. It was a wound that transformed his life forever.

Last, the Apostle Paul applies this lesson of the "divine wound" to all of us in one of the most profound biblical passages: "[God] said to me, 'My grace is sufficient for you, for power is made perfect in weakness.' So, I will boast all the more gladly of my weaknesses, so that the power of Christ may dwell in me. . . . For whenever I am weak, then I am strong" (2 Corinthians 12:9–10). This Scripture passage more than any other has taught me [Bob] about how God works through the brokenness and woundedness of our own humanity. In my own weaknesses, divine power has been revealed—otherwise unreachable areas in my soul and spirit have been deeply transformed and healed.

For men, the grief experience is one of the few things that has the potential to literally dynamite us out of our cultural numbness and businesslike way of relating. It takes a strong man, brave in heart and soul, not to deny or repress or merely cope with grief, but to enter a griefquest, allowing the hurt to transform the deep recesses of his heart. But then perhaps we men have never really understood true courage. Perhaps it lies in heroic inner quests far more than outer prestige, power, success, and wealth.

I consider that the sufferings of this present time are not worth comparing with the glory about to be revealed to us. For the creation waits with eager longing for the revealing of the children of God.

Romans 8:18–19

Notes

1. Four stages of male life drawn from the wisdom of India (quoted in Richard Rohr's *A Man's Approach to God* tape series) are particularly insightful. First, one is a *student*—a learner, taking in and learning from life. Second, one becomes a *householder*—a man marries, raises a family, establishes a household. The problem is that too many men get hung up here, considering this stage the be-all and end-all of life. Their whole life's work becomes building and fixing up their house, then waiting for people to come and visit them. Third, one moves to become a *seeker or forest dweller*—moving out beyond one's own little world to begin to focus on the larger community and world. Last, there is the *wise man or sage*—the man who puts together both inner life and outer life. As the saying goes, he "thinks globally but acts locally." Men like Mahatma Gandhi and Martin Luther King Jr. personify this aspect of the male journey. Few men ever really reach this stage.

2. Rohr describes these stages more simply by naming them *first naiveté*, followed by *complex consciousness*, and finally returning to *second naiveté*. From the outside, it looks like a return to simplicity, and, ultimately, it is. This pattern is at the core of any man's search for meaning and purpose. A man goes out to something new and then ultimately rediscovers something old. Men's psychic journey is essentially an eternal circular journey.

3. A term covering the wide field of woundedness men suffer from their relationships (or lack thereof) with their fathers.

4. Robert Johnson's masterful book *He: Understanding Masculine Psychology* deals entirely with this myth and should be read by every man interested in the "deeper walk" of self-awareness and intimacy with God.

5. Cf. Luke 4:18–19.

6. Cf. Philippians 2:5–11; 2 Corinthians 4:7–18 and 12:7–12.

CHAPTER FIVE

Can the pain of grief ever become healing grief?

Neil's story

Neil could be called the prototypical "jock," a "man's man." Standing 6'8" tall, he is at first sight an intimidating man. He was the starting center for Georgetown University's basketball team in his college days and continues to love all sports to this day. At present, Neil owns and runs a bookstore in Illinois and is happily married with three children. Yet despite his strong masculine image, Neil is a man deeply concerned about relationships, inner spiritual life, and healthy ways of dealing with emotions. His recent experience of a friend's death is a telling story for all men who need to learn how to allow painful grief to become healing grief.

After having experienced three deaths and funerals in a short period of time, Neil wrote:

> How does a man handle grief? . . . Each of these deaths struck me in so many different ways. For Jerry, death was almost a blessing. He was hoping for a miracle, but none came, and he wasted away from 200 pounds to 120. . . . I know that Jerry still lives in Jesus, but it hurts a great deal.
>
> At Diane's funeral, the women were crying, hugging each other, trying to express their many feelings. . . . Most of the men just stood in the funeral home not knowing what to say. All the men were "strong." Most didn't let down their defenses. Some did. . . . Some were able to reach out and hug one another and some were able to cry. But most were the "mighty Warriors." As Robert Moore says, "The Warrior

in his pure form is emotionally detached. . . ." A lot of the men weren't willing to let go, even to the extent of being able to hug Ed (Diane's husband). A firm handshake and a strong pat on the back were their closest contact.

I ask . . . when will men reside more in wisdom and goodness? Why were most of the people at Diane's funeral women? What about the men who weren't there? How can they be confronted by the healing words of Jesus that we heard today? I really feel blessed that I have been able to spend time like I did today. I really wish I would be able to touch some of my friends, to be able to help them let down their guards and see how important the process of grieving is for them.

As I distributed the Eucharist, I was crying over the words to the song "Be Not Afraid." . . . Right in the middle of the song, one of our best friends just reached out and put her hand on my shoulder. I cried then (and ever since when I hear the song). . . . I know I still have a lot to work on, particularly in being more open in expressing my feelings. . . . The reason I was able to cry is because of my relationship with women, especially [my wife] Kathy. Their acceptance of my feelings has taught me much about my masculinity. Perhaps the reason Jesus was able to weep at the death of his friend Lazarus was because he was surrounded by the love of Martha and Mary.

Life is not a problem to be solved, but a mystery to be lived.
Gabriel Marcel

The power of the griefquest process

Neil's story helps answer the question of this chapter. Does the aching pain of grief ever become healing grief? Yes, it certainly can and should if we deal with it properly. Does the healing of grief occur *when* we expect it to, or *how* we plan it, or *in the ways* we suppose it will? Most certainly not.

Perhaps the greatest problem in dealing with grief, loss, and other inner wounds is that we subject them to the same criteria by which we judge all other problems of our life. So often what we men so desperately want is a quick *end result*, not the *process* of getting there. By our nature, and perhaps also by our training, we tend to want immediately to grasp the parameters of the "problem," analyze it coolly and cleanly, and then find an efficient solution or expeditious way to "solve" it. We prefer problems and life in general to be quick, clean, efficient. Unfortunately, our grief-quests will never fit this profile.

The healing of our griefs and losses is achieved not by actually *getting to* a painless place in life but rather by learning to be comfortable *on the road* to healing. In other words, the griefquest itself carries the seeds of healing. The *process* brings the transformation, regardless of whether we actually reach the goal. Facing with honesty what is within, walking with faith, and living with integrity—these are some of the foundation stones that have the power to heal and transform. While we are so busy looking for the light at the end of the tunnel of our hurts, we may ignore the slow, subtle transformations taking place unconsciously as we journey through grief.

Grief is not a stable thing. It is a process. To fully understand the process, it is best . . . to take it apart as much as possible. The [grief] survivor goes through three major phases or reactions during the process. These are Retreating, Working Through, and Resolving. These phases are fluid and overlapping. There is a general progression which must take place to achieve a successful resolution of the loss. . . .

Carol Staudacher, Men and Grief

An old Persian story illustrates this well. A young man went up a mountain, found a cave, and wandered in. He found a pearl of great price in the cave, but it was in the claws of a dragon so overwhelming that he knew there was little chance of getting the pearl. Try as he might, he could not wrest the pearl away and in fact got badly injured in the process of trying. He finally went away with sadness, resigning himself to an ordinary uninspiring life without the pearl. He married, had a family, and worked hard and faithfully for years.

Finally, in his old age, with his children gone and his wife dead, he said, "Before I die, I will go back and look again at the pearl." He found his way back and there was the pearl, as lovely as ever; however, the dragon had shrunk away to almost nothing. The man picked up the pearl and carried it away. He had been fighting the dragon all his life in the practical challenges of daily life. Now he could claim the great prize easily.

This book provides no easy answers or secret remedy for acquiring the "pearl" of peace after grief and loss. What we offer is hope, and stories of hope. Men have survived and grown through great tragedies and pain for generations. In their stories of hope, faith, and courage, we find strength for our own healing process.

In the second section of this book, we will offer two grief-quest aids. First, some foundation stones, some "beacon lights" along the often dark journey. Perhaps you have begun to see the outline of these lights of hope already. Second, we offer stories of our brothers who have walked this road before us.

Neil's story has already pointed the way. His journey from "tough jock" to the gentle, spiritual, open man he is now has been a long, slow transformation. With the help of his wife, with a strong spirituality and committed faith, and with thanks to several powerful weekend experiences and many gentle and patient friends, Neil's griefquest process has blossomed into a blessing for many men, both of us authors included.

The serious problems of life, however, are never fully solved. The meaning and design of a problem seem not to lie in its solution, but in our working at it incessantly.
Carl Jung, "Stages of Life," Modern Man in Search of a Soul

A closing reflection:
What are your patterns of griefquesting?

Just as there are stages of development and growth for men, there are also significant differences in men's reactions and responses to crises in their lives. There are several different levels or patterns to men's griefquests—our attempts to deal successfully with crucial life issues. Healing grief can emerge anywhere along the way, but the degree and depth of healing often depends on successfully negotiating the furthest levels. As might be expected, getting through the various levels depends on a man's commitment to honesty, self-awareness, growth, and spirituality.

As you reflect on the following levels, ask yourself:

◆ Where are you in the process of griefquesting?

◆ Where do you need to grow or be deepened more?

Level 1: Denial—going on as if the loss or grief made no difference at all. This stage is characterized by not only emotional numbness but also a lack of reflective time, inner work, or significant faith response. A man remains the prototypical "John Wayne" or "Marlboro Man"—emotionless, stoic, unaffected by the "weakness" of feelings or grief.

Level 2: Mere coping—making the "minor" life adjustments needed to cope with grief or loss and to get along in now different circumstances. Life is difficult for a while and emotions seem overwhelming briefly, but the man learns to ignore these things and makes subtle lifestyle changes to ease his pain. However, he has not yet dealt with basic issues surrounding the loss or with any negative emotions. His inner consciousness and self-awareness has not progressed much past barely breaking the surface of self-reflection and honesty.

Level 3: Healthy and successful dealing with grief—honestly expressing the negative, challenging emotions of grief and slowly but effectively dealing with the personal turmoil of that loss. He follows Dr. Elisabeth Kübler-Ross's stages[1] successfully, all the way to ultimate acceptance of the situation. This level always takes a period of time to be fully realized. (When my [Bob's] own father died in 1967, it took me nearly eighteen years to fully "put it to rest," and to be at peace with him and his passing.) Although self-consciousness may have begun, grief and loss still may not have penetrated or radically changed the "deep masculine."

Level 4: Wrestling with core life issues—wrestling with one's own spirit, one's God, and the "ultimate questions" of life. His self-awareness becomes greatly increased through long-term faithful reflection, prayer, and inner work. Often a new balance or a profound sense of integration or wholeness emerges deep in his being. Often this stage is reached and entered unconsciously, without an active choice or decision. It simply "happens" when a man is open to the call to move deeper, and when he has a certain integrity of lifestyle, a strong spirituality, and profound self-awareness.

Not reaching this stage does not imply that one has not fully become a man—levels of self-awareness and faith sensitivities differ widely among men. But, as Carl Jung says so well in *Memories, Dreams, Reflections,* "[Though] I cannot blame the person who takes to his heels [at facing these inner trials and struggles] . . . , neither can I approve his finding merit in his weakness and cowardice. . . . I find nothing praiseworthy about such capitulation."

Notes

1. For those unfamiliar with these classic stages of death and dying, they are: (1) Anger, (2) Denial, (3) Bargaining, (4) Depression, (5) Acceptance.

Moving toward healthy male grieving

More healthy male griefquest stories

Minister and writer Robert Schuller tells the story of how as a boy, he and his father watched a tornado destroy the nine buildings of their family farm. Surveying the destruction, the two were awestruck and silent. The elder Schuller was past sixty and had worked hard for twenty-six years to build and pay for his farm. "Twenty-six years, and it's all gone in ten minutes!" he cried. While young Robert remained in the car, his father sifted through the rubble and emerged with a cherished family plaque that read, "Let us keep our eyes fixed on Jesus."

He saw this as a sign from God pointing out a direction for his grief. Discovering an old house in town being torn down, he bought it for $50, dismantled it, and then from those pieces built a new, smaller house on his own farm. Slowly, piece by piece, he added more buildings. Although the tornado destroyed nine farms that afternoon, the elder Schuller was the only farmer to completely rebuild. Grief and loss were transformed by creative action and trust in God.

Joe Scribben, not an outgoing man by nature, had fallen deeply in love with a beautiful young woman, and they were engaged to be married. On the day before their wedding, his fiancée journeyed across the bay near their Canadian home to purchase her wedding dress. Her ship was caught in a terrible storm, and she drowned with all the others on board. In agony and pain, he could only fall on his knees and tearfully cry to God that he had lost "his only friend in the world."

Hours later, when he arose and went downstairs, he found the room filled with friends from the town who embraced him warmly. Joe Scribben was amazed to see how much sympathy and love there was in the world.

Strengthened and deepened by his loss, he gave all his goods to the poor and spent the rest of his life helping those less fortunate. Not an overly religious man, Joe could never have known how his loss would give hope and inspiration to millions when, on one solitary night, he sat in his room and penned the hymn sung around the world: "What a Friend We Have in Jesus." It was grief and loss turned into *life*.

CHAPTER SIX

The healthy male griefquest

"The Chipper" learns about grieving

As a boy he was called "Chipper," and his adult attitude reflected that name. Chip was a healthcare professional used to dealing with crises; he admits he was numb to feelings and had little time for the "darker emotions" of depression or grief. That is, until his beloved twenty-eight-year-old sister was diagnosed with cancer. Unexpectedly, Chip was thrown into a new world, a griefquest world, of turmoil and shock.

> It took a while for my feelings to come out. I felt something but at times wasn't sure what it was. . . . I felt shocked, my mind blank, vulnerable, but not sad or mad. The next months changed from shock to numbness. A certain glaze descended over me so I could do my job, but the verve wasn't there. I had not had to deal with serious change in my life. . . .
>
> My wife and I went for counseling. Our marriage was suffering, and I had a way of assigning some of the stress to her. I think I may have been afraid to go alone. The counselor eventually said to me, "There's no death in your family. You're thirty years old and you've suffered no loss. You haven't had much change in your life either."

Despite his initial resistance to these comments, Chip eventually learned what the counselor meant. He realized he didn't have a framework for dealing with change and coping with loss. During the next three years, he developed a kind of "change strategy."

> I continued in counseling and found out that I am/was a pouter. I wouldn't say much but I'd sulk around the office or

home expecting someone to ask me what was wrong. I really wanted someone to make it better. I visited my sister regularly, but during the end I couldn't go every day. The numbness turned to pain in me. The "Chipper" was hard-pressed to show depression, but I was learning a little bit at a time. I could ask my wife for some time. I could tell her when I was mad or sad. It helped. . . .

Then Chip lost his job, and two days later his sister died. Despite the double grief, his griefquest had progressed to where her funeral could be a truly healing event for him.

My dad called Mom and us together and said, "We all must be strong." Just as quickly as he said it, I found myself blurting out, "Not me!" My wife was terrific. The people who came were terrific. I learned that funerals are for the living . . . that some people have a wonderful way of giving comfort. Others don't. [Back at the house afterwards] the ministers and friends proceeded to entertain us for hours and hours with humorous stories, anecdotes, and joke-telling. Laughing and crying use the same muscles, I'm told. Both were cathartic for me. Much was learned.

Afterward, Chip reflected on the lessons he had learned from the whole experience:

I've learned that there is a process you go through with grief. It doesn't move from one to the other, however. It jumps back and forth. The time period is longer than I thought. Loss we haven't worked through does stick around. It becomes cumulative with other losses in our lives. Once the process of loss begins . . . it becomes an integral part of living.

Defining "healthy grief"

Griefquests do have successful conclusions. Facing griefs and confronting the losses of life in a healthy, uniquely masculine way is possible. Chip's story is a powerful example of the reality that, despite the pain and turmoil a life may be thrown into, a man's experience of grief or loss can become a transforming one. Hope can emerge. Renewal can happen. Life is hard to beat down. With patience, faith, and action, it *can* and *will* reappear and win out.

Chip teaches us a key reality about successful griefquesting— healthy grieving is more a *process* than a *structured program*. It is, as our title indicates, a "quest" for renewed inner peace, acceptance, and balance. The successful griefquest is ultimately something that happens slowly and spontaneously, rather than something we can make happen by our own efforts. There *are* certain key attitudes, however, that seem to mark the successful griefquest and "prime the pump" for healing and hope to emerge.

Within this context, we would define "healthy grief" in this way: *dealing effectively and actively, in a balanced human and spiritual way, with the losses, tragedies, and failures of life.*

This definition covers a wide range of insights and wisdom. Men deal with grief in many ways—beginning with denying its presence and impact. So the first step in any healthy griefquest is "dealing" with the grief "effectively and actively"—not falling into denial, avoidance, or repression. Most men could relate to someone who plants himself in their path and says: "Here I am. I'm not moving. Deal with me or else." It is the same with grief. The turmoil of anger, guilt, loneliness, and sadness surges up within us and demands a confrontation. Unhealthy grief is grief denied and locked within, not expressed or shared. It can have serious ramifications for the unsuspecting, unconscious male.

Dennis was a seventy-two-year-old man married to a younger woman who loved him dearly. They had two small children together, as well as his own older children from an earlier relationship. He was a hardworking man who retired from his job in early 1995, but unfortunately he slowly began to lose his eyesight.

He was depressed for months, totally unable to open up about his struggles with this to anyone, even his wife or several close friends. Though raised Catholic, he practiced no faith. He was a rigidly closed man, isolated and independent, perhaps a paradigm of the "friendless American male." Dennis unfortunately never dealt with or acknowledged his griefs. He committed suicide in his apartment six months after his retirement.

The second phrase of the definition of healthy grief, "in a balanced human and spiritual way," points to the "how" of male griefquests. There are several key elements in a successful griefquest, which serve as guideposts for men struggling through grief and loss:

◆ acceptance of the inner world as valid and real
◆ the need for relationships and the sharing of our stories
◆ creative action and rituals
◆ God and spirituality
◆ personal honesty, awareness, and integrity

In the second half of this book, we will elaborate on these elements, and share examples of how their wisdom has continually been a source of healing for men who have walked the long road of grief before us. We would first like to offer a caveat, however, as to the direction our griefquest will take in these next chapters.

In this book, we hesitate to give structured "steps" to "direct" men through their griefquest. This is not a how-to book for dealing with grief, failure, and loss. There are several reasons for this lack of a highly structured approach, and for our choice to include many stories of brothers grieving their losses.

First, we don't think men (or women) best learn or grow through pain by following someone else's "steps," or by adhering to some predetermined pattern. An organized, methodical approach is helpful in assuring us that what we struggle with is normal, typical, and certainly healable. But personal growth and healing is never linear or logical. It tends to be spontaneous, event-driven, and Spirit-inspired.

Second, we feel that there may not be one single, effective male way of grieving losses. Rather, the truth is that we men are learning together step-by-step how to grieve effectively. Men are literally breaking new ground day by day in learning about themselves, how to deal with emotions and their inner world, what their role and image in society is, and how to relate effectively with women.

Third, we feel stories of our fellow "brothers in God" are the best teachers. The great Rabbi Jesus Christ taught almost entirely in parables and stories. We hope to teach in the best traditions of our ancestors—to pass on the accumulated wisdom of our brothers and allow it to speak to our struggles in this day and age. Let the wisdom of our fellow travelers be the best teacher of all!

CHAPTER SEVEN

Accepting the inner world as valid and real

Terry Smith (1947–70): Lessons from beyond the grave

We expect the old to die, but death seems a cruel thief when it steals the young. Carl Jung says, "It is a period placed before the end of the sentence." In the middle 1960s, a young man entered my life who taught me about death and life long before I was ready to hear about it. The young man's name was Terry Smith.

In August 1964, at the age of fourteen, I entered the Redemptorist Order's high school seminary in Edgerton, Wisconsin. One of my fellow students was a young man who was from my hometown of Grand Rapids, Michigan, named Terry Smith. Although Terry was three years ahead of me, our paths would cross many times: we were in a stage band together (he played lead trumpet), we bowled in a summer seminarian's league, and we played sports together occasionally. In July 1968, I traveled to Clinton, Iowa, for the profession of vows ceremony of some of my friends, and of Terry as well. Upon arriving, I discovered that an accident had happened—while playing soccer two days earlier, Terry had broken his leg and was recuperating in a local hospital.

Though he hoped to soon rejoin his class and make his own profession of vows, it was not to be. Upon further medical tests, the doctors discovered some shocking news—Terry had cancer of the bone. Several months later, he had his left leg amputated well above the knee, and the doctors gave him only about one year to live.

Terry Smith began his own unique grief process then. He was a mere twenty-one years old, with an amputated leg, dealing with the shocking reality of a suddenly shortened life. He did not immediately know what to do with his life, as he wrestled with the weight of what had happened to him. Terry formally left the seminary after leaving the hospital, only to come back again twelve months later in a futile four-day struggle to find his "purpose" in life. Questions, feelings, deep life issues rose up from the depths of his inner world as he entered his own personal agony in the garden.

But it was at this time of his life, a time when many stronger men have fallen to pieces and literally given up on life, that Terry gave his greatest gift to the world. In his time of greatest grief and trauma, Terry Smith chose to let his life take on a unique destiny and great purpose. Always one who loved philosophy and poetry, Terry turned within himself and began keeping a journal of his thoughts, insights, reflections, and poetry. With particular purpose, he entitled it *My Easter Monday*.

A destiny attained

As the physical death of his body progressed, Terry began what he considered his predestined life's work of communicating to as many as he could what life was all about. In *My Easter Monday*, he writes:

> With faith in the whole as my guiding force, I can face anything that happens to me as part of the whole which cannot fail us. The discovery of cancer in my bone which meant amputation and ultimately early death was so bizarre . . . that, due to my basic trust in reality, it had to have been planned, or had to have been as much an integral and necessary part of the whole as all that I had been striving for anyway. . . . I believe even more in all that is now, and must say thanks.

Communicating life became a passion with Terry. Even as he struggled with the inevitable truth of the end that lay ahead, he was consumed with the desire to reach out of himself and give to others the last gift he had—the appreciation of life. One of Terry's journal entries expresses this powerfully:

> Before I die, I must tell myself to someone or to all men. Oh, all you who see, I want you to know that God has walked deep in my soul spreading the sorrows and joys of life. I want you to know that I have longed passionately to walk likewise in the depths of your souls. Allow me to speak the word that God has spent centuries writing. The word is of Christ and of me. It is also of you. The word makes all the words used to make you aware of it superficial and meaningless. Therefore, all who dare to and can believe in visions, I bid you walk with me and breathe together with me. Allow me to tell you myself, and be there when my voice begins to gasp. I need you . . . and you are there.

As he wrestled with approaching death, Terry found himself falling in love. Her name was Bernadette, and she was the sister of a seminary classmate. Though it was a brief relationship, and Terry knew it could not "go" anywhere, it touched and transformed him deeply. An entire section of his journal was dedicated to her, and their love was a powerful inspiration for his unique inner journey. Terry wrote a poem for her entitled "Morning Girl," part of which reads:

> And now, the long-awaited birth
> does fragrance bring to humble earth,
> and birth my task
> does swiftly end
> for from me now your path must wend
> but as you go and I must stay
> remember just
> one yesterday
> remember what
> you surely know
> that once, my love, you touched a soul.

The reality of their unfulfillable future together was a deep and poignant ache for Terry. "I cried a little . . . [but] her words were true and real. . . . I was so overwhelmed by the seeming injustice of my physical handicap." But true to the power and conviction of his inner journey, Terry took much wisdom and strength from their relationship for his own future struggles:

> I still love her deeply. Hopefully I can keep this love in per-spective. I told her once in a letter that if I ever learn how to love, fifty percent of the credit has to go to her. . . . What greater gift can any person give to another? I am forced to stand in gratitude before one person who took the time to let me give to her, and gave so much in return.

During his last months, Terry talked to anyone who would listen. He went into high schools and shared with youth about life and death. He counseled dying people and fellow cancer victims. He shared freely with others during several classes he took at Aquinas College in Grand Rapids. The *Grand Rapids Press* pub-lished articles about him. He wrote poetry and philosophized freely about his faith journey in his touching journal, which even-tually was published.

All of this was Terry's way of letting the world know that his life would not end with death. He had faced his inner demons and emotions and emerged with a wisdom whose origin he freely admitted was elsewhere. He wanted the griefs and losses of his life to have an impact, meaning, and purpose far beyond his short-ened life span. His journal entry for April 10, 1969, says it well: "At my death, speak not of what I was, for you know not. Only be with me and attempt to live my death for your children."

A poem he wrote during that time captured the essence of his attitude toward life in the face of his nearing death:

> Let us not seek
>   to be certain—
>   secure—
>   ever-right-never-wrong-or-wronged.
> Let us charge
>   into the uncertain surf,
> To wrestle
>   the fickle currents.

To swim for our lives
to an Island beyond,
Rather than die dry
on an arid beach.

I personally have a special memory of a time the two of us shared in the summer of 1969. Just weeks before my own entry into novitiate, Terry and I met and went to Pizza Hut for pizza, beer, and poignant conversation. From that long summer afternoon's talk, and two other times I saw him, Terry taught me to confront and never fear death . . . and to live my life fully. Despite my own father's death three years earlier, grief and loss were still relative strangers to me then, and so too was life. It was Terry who made death personal for me and yet also removed the fear from both dying and living. He confidently walked forward into his fear and grief, savoring the ambiguities and mysteries of life throughout. His faith in God, his courage and bravery, his desire to live—these are realities that changed all of us who touched the brief, powerful flame of his existence.

An ending full of symbols

Early in the morning of January 1, 1970, the first day of a brand new year and decade, Terry rang for his nurse in Butterworth Hospital of Grand Rapids. He told her to get his family, for he was going to die that day. Shortly before 3:00 in the afternoon (the same hour another Man died to himself to bring Life to others), he smiled and breathed his last. A short few months before he died, he had written these words:

> What is my life that it should be snuffed out in death? Death terrifies me, but perhaps my greatest agony will be the inability to share this final gift. Perhaps the greatest need of my life will be that someone will listen to my death and understand this light that *seemingly* flickers out. Please be there.
> . . . AND DO NOT ASK WHY I DIED, ASK WHY I SHALL LIVE.

The lesson of Terry Smith's courageous life has great wisdom for men today who face grief, loss, and pain. Let us not ask why there is grief or suffering or loss in our own life, but rather let us ask ourselves where we can find life, hope, and new beginning in the midst of our grief. Perhaps each morning when we awake, all men should cry out with the Terry Smiths of this world, "I WANT TO LIVE!"[1]

"Morals" for modern men

Terry Smith's powerful story highlights one of the greatest difficulties men have. Earlier in this book, we spoke of grief feelings being a foreign world for many men, and also that most men are strangers to their own inner worlds. Most men do not willingly or easily turn within themselves to confront their own hidden motives and feelings, nor do they wade into untouched inner emotional currents without some tremendous incentive.

Terry's life shows us vividly that men can and should accept their inner world as real and valid. The grief and shock of confronting his cancer and approaching death brought Terry into touch with a deep inner level of his being. He moved beyond the ordinary, surface levels of conversation, work, and relating that most men fall into daily. In fact, Terry expressed frustration with the trivialities of most conversations, struck by the great contradiction with his own deep, shattering life issues of cancer, amputation, and death. He said, "Perhaps the greatest need of my life will be that someone will listen to my death and understand this light that seemingly flickers out. . . ."

Terry teaches us men about the depth of insight, feeling, and wisdom in our inner worlds. There are powerful movements, emotions, moods, thoughts, insights, and even true wisdom lying within a man's heart. This is not the exclusive domain of women or "weaklings"—it is, rather, a hidden world of great dynamism and power. Ninety percent of what is within us is pure gold—an undiscovered gold mine that wise men will tap into to become wealthy in wisdom, personal success, and relational happiness.

Unfortunately, we men are so often too busy, too unconcerned, too hardened to begin the task of mining the wisdom within. Terry had the "discomforting grace" of being wrenched into this inner world suddenly by his cancer—but his poise, courage, and composure in bravely befriending that world brought him to a depth of insight at age twenty-three that few men achieve by their eighties.

There are few such great men, however. People seem to fall into these two categories for me: a) the great, b) the small. The small are the vast majority who lack insight. In the overall evolution of mankind, they are important. They are the ones who are moving . . . we all are. The great are those who are DOING the moving. Without them, without someone to attempt to embrace the whole, all the individual parts would crumble. Today, all people must become great.

Terry Smith, My Easter Monday

We men need to discover ways to get in touch with our inner world, to look within, to learn to listen to our inner movements. There are several steps that can help:

1. Accept that you have powerful emotions surging within you. Earlier in this book, we cited a quote by Richard Rohr, who says, "Take away money, sex, and power, and most men on this earth do not know how to motivate themselves. . . ." One author calls us "Numb Men" because of our inability to feel joy or meaning or anything. Because of men's traditional insensitivity or numbness, perhaps the most important step any man might take in life is to become aware that there are forces inside, in his inner spirit and heart, that do have a central place in life. This might mean realizing that

◆ The workplace is only one small part of one's whole existence.

◆ Sexual pleasures are not all there is in life.

♦ Inner forces such as emotion and deeply held values are valid and influential factors for a meaningful life.

♦ There is more to life than what can be seen, heard, tasted, smelled, or "grabbed onto" (in other words, more than what our five physical senses can experience).

Ironically, the first time many men become aware of their inner world is by something that happens to them or by something they did not choose to happen! A man enters a relationship in great expectation and joy, only to discover as time goes by that he is guilty of destructive attitudes or behaviors that he had never been aware of before—but that are obvious to his friend! Or a crisis comes into his family (sickness, children's struggles, and so on), and suddenly nothing seems to make sense anymore. Often only when we men are thrust into a painful, life-shattering situation do we confront inner realities in a serious way.

Eyes must be opened to a new reality. Such an "opening of one's eyes," a revelation, can never be given directly in so many words. We see inner reality only through an "aha" experience, a sudden insight into our own being. There is no way to describe inner reality directly.

John Sanford, The Kingdom Within

Men might be able to touch their inner world by less painful steps, though, if we are only willing to do so. Men can open up that hidden inner life in many ways:

♦ asking a close friend (or spouse) honestly about ourselves

♦ getting away to a quiet place by ourselves—walking, jogging, fishing, or whatever helps us get removed from the world's busyness

♦ personal counseling

♦ reading, study, journaling

♦ prayer, meditation, and reflection times

It took two or three days for the shock of my amputation to wear off. For all my fears, the final look [at my missing leg] was a bit anti-climactic. This sequence proved true over and over again in the next months. Whenever I would be confronted by a new situation to be tried, I would have a great fear . . . but the fear always surpassed the actual event.

Terry Smith, My Easter Monday

2. Identify some of your emotions. (For example, are you driven much by anger, or the need to succeed, or the desire to have power or control, or . . .) Since this may be a confusing point, let me explain briefly the significance of this whole topic for men. Emotions are the interactional building blocks underlying any interpersonal connection that two or more people have. They are common ground both men and women share. Feelings are in themselves neither right nor wrong, they simply *are*. Both sexes have deep, strong feelings present within them—although culturally (and perhaps genetically) men may *express* them differently. Still, feelings are the emotional currents that energize any relationship. Ignoring one's feelings, or denying them, or refusing to listen to them (which happens so often when dealing with grief and loss issues) doesn't make them any less real or valid.

However, too often in relationships, as well as in analyzing themselves, men are *unable* to discover their true feelings about a situation, person, or event. We may have an opinion, or a thought, or a conclusion we have reached "logically"—but these are vastly different from the feelings mentioned above, which are vitally important in any relationship. Thoughts and opinions represent insights or conclusions from the mind and intellect, *not* the heart. These do *not* get to the core of a man's inner world or to his true motivations and heart's condition. A man needs to be able to access and discern the feelings he carries within himself in order to effectively handle grief, love, or any poignant experience.

A concrete suggestion might help men to identify their feelings and emotions (as opposed to their thoughts or opinions). I suggest that most men (and women too) could benefit by using a rule known as the "Think-Feel Rule." Ask yourself the simple question: "How do I feel?" and then state your answer in this sentence form: "I feel _____." If, when you state this feeling, you can substitute "I think" for "I feel," and it still makes sense, *it is not a feeling but a thought, opinion, or judgment.* For example, "I feel that this is an uplifting experience" is a personal opinion, not a feeling. "I feel uplifted and encouraged" is a true statement of inner feelings.[2]

Most of a man's problems come from his not being able to sit quietly in his chamber.

Pascal

---

3. Determine how your moods and emotions affect your everyday life and relationships. Moods and emotions are subconscious motivating factors affecting many if not all human events, interactions, and relationships. When we've had a stressful argument with a loved one at home, or prolonged financial strains, or the death or loss of an especially close friend—it is inevitable that our work or professional life will also be affected. The reverse is true as well—how many men and women tend to bring home the stresses and tensions of their workplace? A man would be foolish to presume that he is an emotional rock, totally unaffected or unmoved by these powerful and emotional forces within him. The challenge for men is to become aware of *how* significant these forces are and how they tend to affect other areas of their life. As Jesus Christ says wisely, "You will know the truth, and the truth will make you free" (John 8:32).

One of the best ways to confront inner issues and feelings is entering and remaining in a serious and honest relationship with a significant other. In any honest, open, and committed relationship, we will sooner or later be forced to confront stubborn areas within ourselves! Sincere love relationships can be the most challenging yet rewarding experiences we will ever have in life. It is not surprising that Terry himself struggled through a deep love relationship during the last year of his life. Though it wounded him, it also opened him up to the knowledge and transforming experience that only a beloved can do.

---

sorrow is good
to share our sorrow is better
if we could
        Terry Smith, My Easter Monday

In conclusion . . .

Ultimately, perhaps it is so difficult for men (and women) to get in touch with their inner world because the path to the riches of that world is a solitary one. Though companions may lend support, no one can make the journey for us—we must walk there alone, led onward by quiet courage and a desire for wholeness and peace, inspired by a still, small Voice within that gives us hope. Many men are so afraid of aloneness that they never begin this journey. But in the quiet moments of walking the path within oneself, men can begin to unearth the "pearl of great price." The rewards of turning within are well worth the challenges. For within oneself lie untapped, many-faceted treasures: answers, intuitions, insights, hidden energy, and wisdom.

The great Swiss psychologist Carl Jung wrestled with the inner journey most of his life. A quote from his famous autobiography sums up well the challenge of this journey:

> The man who . . . steps beyond the limits of the intermediary stage truly enters the "untrodden, untreadable regions" where there are no charted ways and no shelter spreads a protecting roof over his head.
>
> Insights into the dangers and painfulness of such a state may well decide one to stay at home, that is to never leave

the safe fold and warm cocoon, since these alone promise protection from inner stress. Those who do not have to leave father and mother are certainly safest with them. A good many persons, however, find themselves thrust out upon the road. . . . In no time at all they will become acquainted with the positive and negative aspects of human nature.

I cannot blame the person who takes to his heels at once. But neither can I approve his finding merit in his weakness and cowardice.[3]

Finally, in his own parable fashion of teaching, Jesus himself speaks of the beauty and ultimate value the inner quest can bring. In images that have become quoted through the generations, Jesus reminds us that the things of greatest value in life are worth the greatest effort:

The kingdom of heaven is like treasure hidden in a field, which someone found and hid; then in his joy he goes and sells all he has and buys that field. Again, the kingdom of heaven is like a merchant in search of fine pearls; on finding one pearl of great value, he went and sold all that he had and bought it. (Matthew 13:44–45)

Today our lives must part, but in your hand—like mine—remains a heart, the center of all our yesterdays, which we now gather for tomorrow—when we will kiss again within the embrace of the God I take leave to go and meet.

Terry Smith, May 10, 1969

Notes

1. My thanks and support to Mrs. Mary Smith, Terry's mother, for her permission and support in retelling Terry's story.

2. Examples of *feeling words* would be angry, embarrassed, quiet, talkative, lonely, happy, appealing, distant, surprised, threatened, comforted, hopeful, confident, jealous, alarmed, loved, etc. Feeling words are adjectives following the construction "I feel . . ."

3. Carl Jung, *Memories, Dreams and Reflections* (New York: Vintage Books, 1965), pp. 344–346.

CHAPTER EIGHT

The need for relationships

A friend is one to whom you may pour out all the contents of your heart, chaff and grain together, knowing that the gentlest of hands will take it and sift it, keep what is worth keeping, and with a breath of kindness, blow the rest away.

Arabian proverb

"When you can't come back": The Dave Dravecky story

Baseball fans will remember the name Dave Dravecky. He was a San Francisco Giants baseball pitcher in the late 1980s who gained quite a reputation for his pitching ability and skill. He contracted cancer in that pitching arm, however, immediately putting his career in jeopardy. Dave's courageous battle against cancer is recounted in a book entitled *When You Can't Come Back* (Zondervan). In this book, he speaks of the depression and grief he faced, and the ultimate sacrifice he had to make in having his pitching arm amputated due to the cancer. The magnitude of this loss was amplified by the fact that he was a professional baseball player, who had made his career out of the skillful use of his arm. Dave reflects about this loss, saying:

> My arm was to me what hands are to a concert pianist, what legs are to a ballerina, what feet are to a marathon runner. It's what people cheered me for, what they paid their hard-earned

money to see. It's what made me valuable, what gave me worth, at least in the eyes of the world. Then suddenly that arm was gone.

Dave and his wife, Jan, were both plunged into the depths of despair and grief. He freely admits that relationships were key to surviving the grieving process. Though the crisis severely strained Dave and Jan's relationship for a while, words from his doctor challenged him to a new perspective: "You know, the two of you, it's unbelievable that you're still married. Both of you are working with such deficits, and you're both hurting. [To Dave] Your wife needs help and she needs it now. . . ." The two of them began focusing on the important things in their life—time with each other, their kids, and God. Dave shares some of the lessons he learned along the way:

> Now instead of denying the losses in my life, I'm learning to express them. Instead of throwing phones against the wall, I'm learning to listen to the person on the other end of the line. Now I'm beginning to learn something about emotions. . . . [I am] learning how to express my needs and receive love from other people.

Be slow to fall into friendship; but when thou art in, continue firm and constant.

Socrates

In times of grief, men need relationships

At its core, any man's griefquest is a solitary journey. Some pains in life can only be confronted and dealt with by a man himself. But there should be no doubt that *men need others* to accompany them on their griefquests. The pain and turmoil may be uniquely theirs to own and honor, but a successful griefquest is rarely ever made alone. Men in pain need companionship, support, and encouragement from other men and women.

This may seem like an obvious statement—one that few men would dispute. But although men talk a good game about friendship, few of them truly know or do much about it. This is not the place to reflect on what David Smith calls the "friendless American male" mystique. But let me say at least that I believe most men have serious problems with allowing and enabling friendships in their lives. Many reasons have been offered for this: intrinsic male competitiveness, mistrust, aversion to showing emotions, fear of intimacy, inadequate role models, inability to ask for help. All are valid and relevant.[1]

For men reading this book, these social facts may be interesting and relevant, but they are ultimately tangential to our purpose here. All we need to know right now is an undeniable and immutable truth that thousands of men before us have already learned: *In times of pain, we men need friendships where there is understanding, support, and encouragement, and relationships where we can share our story.* How we do this—with whom, in what ways, what words we choose—is not as important as the actual doing.

There are at least two good reasons why relationships are essential in times of grief and loss. First, we need other people to affirm our own quest and to validate what we are going through. Many people, and certainly our culture as a whole, find the inner work of griefquesting completely useless and nonproductive.

Part of your own being may deny the impact of negative emotions and downplay their role in your life. Talking with another person honors the reality and impact of grief in your life, and affirms that you are acting wisely in confronting and dealing with it.

The better part of a man's life consists of his friendships.
Abraham Lincoln

Second, relationships and friendships teach us the value of "mud-sitting." It is absolutely vital to have someone to "sit in the mud" with you when you are grieving. Before you think I am crazy, allow me to share the story behind this point.

There was a farmer who was out plowing his field one spring morning. The spring thaw had just occurred, and there were many muddy valleys in the field. Eventually his tractor became stuck in the mud, and the harder he tried, the deeper he got stuck. Finally he asked his neighbor for help, and the neighbor came to look over the situation. He shook his head and then said, "It doesn't look good, but I'll give it a try—pulling you out. But if we can't get it out, *I'll come sit in the mud with you.*"

Mud-sitting may be the best thing one friend can do for another in times of grief and loss. We cannot take away the pain or loss. We should not downplay it or pass it off lightly ("Don't worry, you'll be okay . . ."). But what we can do is *sit in the mud with our friend*—just be there for that person, be present emotionally, spiritually, and perhaps physically.

Men can probably grow through grief without close friendships, but with them the quest becomes lighter and smoother, the journey less fearful and alarming.

Going about looking as if we are totally self-reliant and independent and don't need anything from anyone is a facade hiding a deep longing for intimacy.

Jerry Greenwald

Fatherhood denied—Jack's grief

Jack is a man who freely admits he has been blessed in many ways. He is a longtime substance-abuse counselor, has been happily married for fourteen years, and has a faith that is central in his life. But he was unprepared for the grief that entered his life when he found out he and his wife were unable to conceive a child. Doctor visits confirmed that "about everything that could be wrong was." His body had too many problems for physical fatherhood.

It was a heavy burden for Jack, one that triggered other old doubts about himself and his masculinity:

> It was a difficult period for me, more because I've always felt I was different from other men I associated with in high school and college. I didn't feel I measured up to their standards somehow, especially in how they appeared to relate to women.
>
> When I discovered I had this problem in my body, it was like the last straw. I had tried to run from my insecurities about women and my manhood for years through alcohol and drugs—but this was a problem in my own body, and I could no longer run from it.
>
> It was a very painful period. . . . There were many times when I was so angry coming back from the doctor. It affected my relationship with Joan for a period of time—both emotionally and sexually. At times I felt abandoned by God. . . . I was hurt and angry.

From the outside, you never would have known what Jack was going through. His job continued, as did his marriage, church life, and the other basics of his life. But within himself, Jack knew he needed to reach out for help.

> Then I spent a great deal of time talking with men I know in my church who had to adopt children themselves. I was surprised how many men there were who had been through this already. I talked with several priest friends of mine. And most of all, I spent time talking with my wife, Joan, about all this. . . . By doing these things, I worked through some of the pain and anger. I realized that Joan and I were not alone, that there were other people who had gone through this before . . . , that there were many people willing to help talk about it . . . , and that Joan's love for me would not change. Soon after that, we decided to consider adopting. . . .

Jack and Joan adopted two beautiful children. Today Jack speaks gladly of how God worked through the whole process, bringing him to healing and new life:

> It did not work when I tried to "stuff" everything, not talk about it, trying to handle it all on my own without expressing my anger and hurt. I have learned the wisdom of talking about my problems with others—physical problems, sexual problems, emotional problems, even feelings. Other men helped me, and my wife helped me immensely. God has done a great healing in me, and in us! He has blessed us with two beautiful children. . . .

A man must get friends as he would get food and drink for nourishment and sustenance.

Randolph S. Bourne

The intimate relationships of our life

Intimacy is not easy for men. Many men not only do not know how to be intimate, but are afraid of opening up to a significant other (spouse, close friend) for fear they will "lose something" of themselves. One man said it well: "With any partner, including my former wife, I've been scared to show too much of myself for fear that I would somehow lose myself and my manhood. I've hidden a lot of feelings and needs, trying to remain invisible. . . ."[2] Yet most men do realize their need for intimacy, love, and affection, and this need is never stronger than at crisis times.

T. S. Eliot says that a person's spouse "is a still point in a turning world." These words are never truer than at difficult times. A spouse or an intimate friend can be a quiet rock of strength . . . a source of support and encouragement . . . a calming, stabilizing presence . . . a catalyst for self-honesty and personal expression . . . a "sponge" for emotional venting . . . a probing voice knowing our inner workings all too well.

I work with men under stressful situations. These guys don't know how to express emotions. My wife has taught me to bring my feelings out. I'm a better man today because of her. She really cares about me. Without her love and genuine concern for my welfare, I'm sure I'd be a very different person. Maybe it's the little boy that remains in all men, i.e., we need to constantly have the support of the women we love.

David Smith, The Friendless American Male

Deep within, most men are afraid of loneliness and rejection, feelings that routinely occur with grief and loss. The necessary wounding of grief can force us into our deepest fears and insecurities. An intimate friend is able to see those things we do not want to be seen—and accept us all the same.

Any relationship of depth, intimacy, or true love involves risk. It is a risk opening up—we risk rejection, misunderstanding, the normal tensions when friendship progresses beyond the "honeymoon" stage. For many men, it is a risk to share the grief feelings surging within. These emotions may not be "organized" or controllable; tears may come. These feelings certainly will not be logical or able to be structured and then removed. We may need to give ourselves permission to be "weak," or out of control, or emotional.[3]

Grief can severely test intimate relationships, particularly if there have been hidden problems up to that time. The pressure cooker of personal turmoil and loss can force to the surface long-buried tensions and fears. This is yet another reason to do "relationship work"[4] *before* a crisis comes; then a man is far better equipped when it does come. But if your griefquest puts your intimate relationship to a severe strain, we recommend seeing a counselor or trusted clergyman for advice and help. Struggles in intimate relationships are very typical when stress or loss occurs in a person's life.[5]

Sometimes wordless hugs or physical embraces can be the most powerful means of support possible. Listening without judgment or without demanding answers is likewise a key. Above all, men in grief need *encouragement* from the intimates of their life—encouragement to take the risk of sharing, to affirm their self-esteem, and to continue on their griefquest with hope and trust, knowing they are not alone.

Job loss and transfer—Ken's griefquest

Ken is a father of five children, grandfather to five more, and had been married for almost forty years. He worked hard all his life to provide for his family, and slowly rose at his job to a position of sales engineer with direct account responsibility. His territory covered five states, generating sales of over one million dollars annually. Ken's griefquest began when management decided his expertise was needed in the inside office as a backup for the outside salesmen. The job change meant a loss of commissions and travel for Ken, as well as status and position.

> My finances and feelings both were hurt. It even got worse. Promises of "higher status" were not kept, and I was on the level with non-degreed employees. Additional work was dumped on me and pressure was increased. I was emotionally drained overnight. My grief was increased twenty months later when my poor performance merited probation with possible job loss. I could not believe what was happening to me.

Ken's grief was compounded by the onset of some health problems that his wife was experiencing, problems that would lead eventually to her death by cancer. Basically a very balanced and sensitive man, Ken found these griefs extremely difficult to deal with:

> I had a lot of anxiety and feelings of insecurity. . . . My emotional balance was severely upset. I had to continually guard against friends sharing their own negative attitudes—

especially a coworker who was going through the same thing (probation). It took effort not to let his feelings of anger and resentment add to my own. . . . Hearing negative things does not help.

Ken shared with me what a difference his wife, Cathy, had made in coping with his grief:

Being able to share with Cathy on a regular basis just how the job was going and my feelings of anger and anxiety was a tremendous help. She lifted my spirits by continuing to affirm my worth and encourage my positive reaction to hurtful situations. She not only helped me meet challenges put before me, but assured me of her support if the pressure became too great. "Don't worry—with God's help we'll make it through, even if we have to sell the house," she would always say.

Sharing with other male friends who had suffered similar losses was a great blessing. Some were older and had already passed through the hard times. Others were in the midst of the struggle just as I. Advice, encouragement, feelings, prayers—these were all shared. I realized I was experiencing something very common—I was not alone; I was not singled out as a failure. Some even attended support groups and encouraged me to do the same if I felt the need.

Finally, Ken's strong faith was a rock of strength for him:

Accepting God's grace and gifts and bringing them to mind again and again—this helped me keep perspective. God was going to save me from this situation. For my own good, I needed to forgive those who had wronged me . . . but I don't remember being able to do that right away!

Ken's job performance not only eventually improved, but he surprised his bosses by the positive reports he continued to receive from different departments. They were amazed he had turned it around and wondered how he did it. Ken's griefquest now leads him to say freely, "Grief and loss are best handled by how you live out each day, whether there is sickness or health, grief or joy, in good times or bad. I thank God always. . . ."

We are all born for love; it is the principle of existence and its only end.

Benjamin Disraeli

Sharing your griefquest with other men

In Jack's and Ken's stories, you may have noticed that talking with other men played a major role in helping them to deal with their grief effectively. Through sharing their struggles with other men, they received much-needed affirmation that their own singularly masculine pain was not unique, that others had felt the same griefs, and that they would emerge from the foreign land of inner emotional pain to be strong and healthy again.

This type of support and encouragement is tremendously helpful for hurting men. How males support one another in times of grief and loss will be different from our female counterparts. For the majority of men, independence and autonomy are key elements in their psyche because, unfortunately, most men grow up without the network of close relationships marking many women's lives. Steven Farmer describes it well when he says, "There are three barriers that interfere with deeper friendships with other men: competitiveness, distrust, and fear of intimacy."[6] Yet despite these inherently friendship-defeating attitudes we've grown up with, men deep within are starved for friendship. The lonely and friendless gaps within us cry out for filling and nourishing, in spite of problems of cultural conditioning and upbringing.[7] When grief sets in, the cry becomes stronger and perhaps sadder, because of the horrible lack of male friendship most men experience.

Thus, there is something unique and powerful in the support and affirmation that other men can contribute when a man is on a personal griefquest. It might be described as "supportive autonomy"—*acknowledging* a brother's pain, *supporting* him in words and even action, but *respecting his autonomy* and independence of action. A key attitude here for the grieving male is *availability*—

making time and room in his life for men to get close to his pain, instead of walling it off with stoic, "tough guy" hardness. Another key attitude is *risk*—taking the chance of opening up, being vulnerable for a moment, sharing his pain with a man he can trust (perhaps a fellow worker, a member of his church, a trusted friend).

A man could invite a friend out for coffee or a beer, or to his house or apartment for a visit, and then say simply: "I know you went through a difficult time with such and such. I have always respected your opinion and insights. . . . So, what worked for you in your pain?" As mentioned before, some men find that a counselor, therapist, or clergyman can be helpful in venting their frustrations and hurt and in seeking new direction and balance. Men need to relearn a basic lesson of life: It is not a sign of weakness to ask for help.

> *But men may learn best about masculinity from the company of other men. They experience there the obvious things: bravado, aggressiveness, competition, ribald humor, braggadocio. But if they are lucky, and travel in the right circles, they will learn much more: about quiet strength, keeping their word, respecting the law, thinking for themselves, sticking to their guns, standing for principle, watching out for the "little guy," respecting women and laughing at themselves.*
> Patrick Arnold, SJ, America *magazine, 7 October 1989*

Travels with Beatrice— A closing lesson from Dante's "Inferno"

In his classic work *The Divine Comedy*, Dante uses an image that contains great wisdom for men. In that work, his image of feminine beauty is a woman named Beatrice, whom he saw when he was nine years old. When, guided by Beatrice, Dante travels through hell and purgatory and finally reaches heaven, he curiously never looks directly at God. Instead, he just looks at Beatrice and Beatrice looks at God. Right at the end of his famed journey, he comes to know God on *her* face. Dante continues looking at her and comes to true wisdom of his God. In that great scene, all creation and all love become as one for him. He has achieved life's perfection.

Dante later writes of that experience, saying, "The spirit of life, which has its dwelling in the secret chambers of the heart, began to tremble so violently that my body shook and in trembling said these words, 'Behold, a deity stronger than I is coming to rule me.'" From that time on, Dante writes, "love quite governed my soul."

This story is a perfect example of how a man needs another special person to help him reach God. No man ever reaches wholeness or salvation or happiness by himself, for we men are social by nature. In and through Beatrice, Dante sees the face of God. In relationships with our "beloveds," or with those closest to our heart (our children or closest friends), we too suddenly find the veil of the Divine lifted and God appearing. We need these loved ones in our life, even if the potential for hurt or for losing them is a shadow looming in the background. Through the Beatrices of our life, "a deity stronger than I is coming to rule" us.

Notes

1. If you are interested in further reflections in this area, I recommend the following books: *The Friendless American Male*, by David Smith (Regal Books, 1983); *Why Can't Men Open Up?* by Steven Naifeh and Gregory Smith (Warner Books, 1984); *The Wounded Male*, by Steven Farmer (Ballantine Books, 1991). More and more is being published in this area today, such as *You Just Don't Understand*, by Deborah Tannen (Morrow, 1990) and *Men Are from Mars, Women Are from Venus*, by John Gray (HarperCollins, 1992).

2. Steven Farmer, *The Wounded Male* (New York: Ballantine Books, 1991), p. 155.

3. See chapter twelve for some exercises to help with this.

4. "Relationship work" refers to the basic elements needed to establish and maintain a successful, honest, loving, intimate relationship with another person. We would consider these elements to be basic: open and honest communication in every key area; spending quality time to-

gether; equality and shared responsibility for growth in love; faithfulness and a shared faith framework for the relationship; avoiding destructive behaviors and attitudes, such as jealousy, possessiveness, holding onto anger and resentments; arguing not to "win" but to improve the relationship.

5. Studies have shown that ninety percent of bereaved couples are in serious marital difficulty within months after the loss of their child. This happens primarily because of the inability to share grief (Harriet Schiff, *The Bereaved Parent*, p. 90).

6. Farmer, op. cit., p. 117.

7. Many of the cultural patterns today's men have developed center around their intrinsic (but unexpressed) hunger for male support and friendship—e.g., watching sports together, drinking together in bars, hunting, and so on. I suspect that much of the psychological framework behind male-only clubs, and the resistance to changing those structures, derives at least partially from a deep desire to bond with their brothers apart from the "distracting" influence of women.

CHAPTER NINE

Creative action and ritual

Transforming grief into action

In 1667, a man named Simon Pereins found himself thrust into a nearly hopeless situation. He was arrested by the Spanish Inquisition and thrown into a dungeon cell. Being found guilty by the Inquisition in those days was tantamount to a death sentence. No one was ever released. The best a man could hope for was to linger on in a cell that was dark, damp, and full of bugs, until death finally released him.

Who knows what feelings crossed Pereins's mind? Certainly anger and depression, perhaps helplessness and grief. But Simon Pereins chose instead to take action in the face of disaster. Using clay from his cell floor mixed with some of his food, he made paint. Then, taking fragments of cloth, strings, and straw from his clothes, blanket, and floor, he made a crude paintbrush. He then used his cell door as a canvas, and on that door he painted a picture of the Virgin Mary and the Child Jesus. The picture was so beautiful that his inquisitors were convinced he had seen a heavenly vision. They set him free. That painting still exists; it is now called the *Altar del Pardon (Altar of Pardon)*.

Simon Pereins's story is one of positive attitude and constructive action in the face of tragedy and grief. It is healthy masculinity at its best.

The Cree Indians of northwest North America have a custom called the tree-wounding ritual. The story of a man named Jaque illustrates this ritual. After his brother died suddenly, Jaque was torn by sadness and anger. So, following ancient custom, he went into the forest, selected a tree, and, after uttering a prayer, stripped away a piece of the bark. Now the tree, like Jaque, had lost something whose loss caused deep pain. Many times over the following months, Jaque returned to visit the tree. As the seasons passed, the wound in the tree healed. So did the wound in Jaque's heart. With the tree as a visible reflection of his loss, Jaque was reminded that he, too, was healing.

Jaque's tree-wounding ritual (referred to by Maryland psychotherapist Thomas Golden)[1] is another healthy masculine way of dealing with the inner turmoil of grief and loss.

These active rituals [or actions] . . . perform the same function as crying and talking about one's grief. They provide a safe place to immerse oneself a bit at a time in the chaos of the grief.
Thomas Golden, Different Paths Toward Healing

The healing power of creative ritual

Both of these stories reflect a deep wisdom for men struggling through grief. In these stories (and in most others in this book), we find that men seem to best work through their grief by utilizing *creative actions or rituals* to further their griefquest. Certain masculine energy and power are released by concrete actions and rituals that can put a man in touch with the hidden grief feelings within himself.

Grief counselor Tom Golden writes that feelings of anger, guilt, sadness, and helplessness comprise the bulk of masculine grief. Healing these feelings can only be accomplished by processing the grief a little at a time. Few griefs and losses, and certainly not those that terribly uproot our lives, are easily dealt with or quickly healed. Crying, expressing tears, over the griefs of life is certainly effective and helpful, as is being able to talk about them openly. These are probably the most efficient ways to work through our grief. The problem, however, as we've discussed previously, is that many men seem not to be instinctively good at either talking or shedding tears. Our upbringing, cultural expectations, lack of contact with the inner self, and the roles we feel we have to play for others (children, wives, family, friends, and so on) tend to block the free expression of tears or talking through the feelings of anger, guilt, sadness, and helplessness mentioned by Golden.

So, in times when grief feelings dominate and overwhelm us, our instinctive tendency may be to find safety in an area where we generally are more comfortable—taking action, striving for goals, "controlled aggressiveness" (as John Sanford phrases it). Robert Moore, Patrick Arnold, and other men's-movement writers today speak of this part of men, calling it the "warrior energy." They go on to say that men tend to need their activity (warrior energy) to put them in a safe place to experience the griefs they feel. Far from being in denial of what has happened to them (as some think), this action-oriented behavior can open men up to acknowledge and honor the griefs within.

In other words, instead of confronting their "weaknesses" (in this case, grief feelings) directly, men would be wiser to use their instinctual strengths to deal with them. Taking creative action or engaging in some uniquely personal ritual can be very healing for men, as long as there is a conscious link made between the action and the loss. As Golden says well, "Every time a man performs the action, it activates the grieving process and moves it toward healing. The important aspects are that you do it consciously (intentionally—not let it happen to you), and that you in some way honor and acknowledge your grief in the process."[2]

◆ What is your hurt, grief, or loss? Is it connected to a person with whom you have shared memories or interests? Is it related to a job, illness, or loss that evokes other memories?

◆ Take time to brainstorm possible actions, motions, memorials, projects, physical activities, hobbies, or rituals that you could connect or relate to this grief.

Nolan Richardson, the head coach of the Arkansas national basketball team, was asked after the final game about his daughter who had died some years prior. He replied that after each game won, as he walked out of the arena, he said to her, "Baby, we got you another one." Richardson had connected his grief over his daughter with his greatest skill, being a basketball coach.
    Thomas Golden, Different Paths Toward Healing

Using creative actions or rituals to get in touch with loss and grief certainly does not mean that men cannot or should not use their relational skills to heal their grief. Golden and other professional counselors all express the tremendous value of talking and of open emotional expression:

> We are painting with broad strokes if we attempt to link men with action and women with relating. In general men tend toward action as a primary mode in healing their grief while using relating as secondary, and women are the opposite. What we are describing are tendencies, not hard and fast rules about a man's way versus a woman's way.[3]

What makes an action or ritual healing?

One of the greatest barriers to healthy human openness in expressing emotional pain is the learned and cultural patterns of relating we grew up with. These blocks prevent many men and women from acknowledging and honoring their inner woundedness.
    Creative actions and rituals can enable deeper healing to begin by reminding us subconsciously of old relationship patterns. Actions and rituals are condensed expressions of these old patterns, and re-enacting old or freely chosen new rituals can help put us in touch with deep, unresolved feelings.
    One man places a ceramic angel on top of his Christmas tree every year. He remarks:

I took that angel after my mother died. It belonged to her—my dad gave it to her their first Christmas. They had always put it on the tree after Midnight Mass. It meant that Christmas had come. I haven't gone to Midnight Mass for years, but every December 24th at midnight, I put that angel on the tree, and I think of my parents, and just that angel brings back all the Christmases in my mind.[4]

Healthy actions and rituals also embrace the two harshest realities of any grief or loss: that *something has changed forever,* and that whether you like it or not, *life goes on.* Constancy and change—holding these two opposing energies in healthy balance is a difficult task. Rituals and actions have the ability to embrace both the constancy of life and the painful transformation that grief brings into life. Good rituals and well-chosen actions can contain *both* these incongruities.

For example, being a priest for twenty-two years, I can speak firsthand of the tremendous power that the funeral service has in bringing healing, closure, and renewal to mourners. The Catholic funeral rite, when done in a personal and attentive manner, is a powerful blend of structured certainty (the formal prayers and rites) and the uniquely personal (memories, anecdotes, Scriptures, songs specially chosen and blended into the service).

Even though the funeral of my wife was the hardest thing I've ever gone through, something about the Mass and funeral service really touched me. I heard the words of hope and resurrection like I never had before. The pain of her being gone still hurt worse than anything . . . but after those services, I was able to finally let go of her. . . . I trusted that she was in a far better place, and that I could go on—with her up there watching out for me!

A sixty-three-year-old man after burying his wife

In their fine book *Rituals for Our Times*, Evan Imber-Black and Janine Roberts speak of the five purposes of rituals.[5] A good grief ritual or action should always take into account these essential realities:

◆ **Relating**—expressing that there has been a significant relationship in our life, whether with a beloved person, a job, or some specific reality that has impacted our life

◆ **Changing**—acknowledging or marking that a transition or change has occurred in this relationship[6]

◆ **Healing**—honoring our attempts and desire to recover from the loss or grief we have experienced. Since all healing takes time, this may for a while consist simply of "sitting in one's grief," being open to growth or healing through God, time, others, and self.

◆ **Believing**—voicing personal foundational beliefs and finding a "meaning" behind the loss. Often grief and loss make people realize that they have nothing that they really do believe in, or else they realize that what they believe is too shallow. "What do I really believe?" can be a significant question at this time.

◆ **Celebrating**—expressing joy and gratitude, honoring life with festivity. It may seem strange at first to "celebrate" grief, but it is important to honor and celebrate the role and impact that the "missing reality" has had in our life. Celebration can be an extremely freeing way of bringing to light previously buried thoughts and feelings.

In chapter seven, I introduced you to Terry Smith, the young man whose cancer and death so influenced my own teenage life. During the last year and a half before his death, Terry's life was a perfect example of these five realities in action. He never denied or ran from the harsh reality of death facing him. Rather, in acknowledging the truth and reaching out to other people, his creative actions brought healing to many. He celebrated life and his core beliefs in all his activities those final months—from falling in love, to teaching high school kids, to counseling other cancer victims and hospital patients, to the interviews he did for the *Grand Rapids Press*, *Detroit Free Press*, and others.

Terry was a young man who undertook healthy, life-giving actions when confronted with the grief of cancer's "death sentence" upon him. Creative action was his response to cruel fate. Though he died at the young age of twenty-three, his life and death provide a perfect pattern for male griefquesting. Healthy, creative actions and rituals are one of men's most powerful tools for healing grief.

The "ritual void" of modern society

Before moving on to specific suggestions for creative actions and rituals, I want to say a few words about the lack of rituals in our world today. We live in a culture that minimizes and de-emphasizes ritual. We Americans pride ourselves on being free from cultural rituals, such as the trappings of royalty (in England), or precise traditional codes of etiquette and protocol (as in Japan). We tend to view ourselves as being down to earth, independent, free from any thing or structure that ties us down. (Are you old enough to remember Frank Sinatra's modern-day credo, "I've Gotta Be Me" or the song "Don't Fence Me In!"?)

Some of us men grew up with very few family rituals, or with minimalized rituals. If we did not attend church as children, for example, it's likely that the practice and structure of organized religion today may seem too confining. Some men grew up with rigid, highly prescribed family customs, or even obligatory, possibly imbalanced types of rituals (for example, forced, uncomfortable visits to "Uncle Charlie's" or "Aunt Agnes's").

Thus, the problem for some of us is that we *do not place a high value on personal rituals or creative actions.* We may not have many in our own personal life. Our culture as well has few "blessed" rituals to deal with grief, and the few there are (funerals, wakes, and so on) are viewed as unpleasant chores that must be done whether we like it or not!

I'm not afraid of funerals—I just don't want to be there when it happens to me!

Woody Allen

Robert Fulghum, the author of *All I Really Need to Know I Learned in Kindergarten*, has written a new book *(From Beginning to End)* dealing exclusively with the value of rituals in our lives. In this book, he uses many anecdotes and stories to show that rituals are extremely important for us in that they bring a sense of order and structure to our lives. "The reason for all these rituals is that we cannot live with chaos. We have a hunger and need for what you could call an automatic pilot."[7]

I hear and I forget.
I see and I remember.
I do and I understand.
Confucius

In Fulghum's own personal life, the rituals connected with his griefs and losses had a powerful effect. He used to take off from work on the birthday of his daughter (given up for adoption early in their marriage) to think about her and wonder where she was. After the success of his first book, the daughter learned of his identity, and the two had an emotional reunion. Until recently, Fulghum reveals, he avoided discussing his death or funeral with his wife or four children. Following a long talk, his children decided he should have a grave plot near where they lived. After buying it, Fulghum watched them dig the hole, then replace the dirt. "Now I have a physical location that reminds me that I have a limited amount of time," Fulghum writes. "When I have a lousy day or am unfocused, I'll stop by there and think about what's really important. One day I even lay on the grave. . . . I felt very comfortable, like I was part of this unbelievable mystery."

Practical griefquesting activities for men

It is vital for men to find meaningful rituals and creative actions to deal with their pains, losses, and griefs. In *Rituals for Our Times*, the authors speak of the importance of planning this whole process. They mention five elements that could be helpful to men thinking of doing rituals or activities—*preparation, people, place, participation, and presents*.[8] The use of personally meaningful *symbols* or *symbolic actions* or *objects* can also be powerful. Symbols have a meaning all their own—they speak without words, and they subtly but surely connect us to the past.

But there are already many powerful activities and rituals available to interested men. Since one purpose in writing this book is to share the accumulated wisdom of our brothers throughout the world experiencing and dealing with grief, we would like to offer some tested and true suggestions:

1. Letter writing. As a way to express farewells, or to "speak" the painful feelings that are hard to say out loud, writing a letter can be one of the most powerful and effective tools available for men. You could write either a good-bye letter (verbalizing your painful loss), or a feelings letter (expressing the feelings and thoughts you have about the grief). Addressing it to the person or subject of your grief but not sending it gives an element of freedom and release to your writing. Memories can be recalled, anger and hurts verbalized, unspoken feelings or wounds expressed in a constructive fashion.

What you do with the letter after finishing it is also significant—for example, consciously and symbolically destroying it or preserving it to reread from time to time. The letter by then has become a receptacle or a precious container for your grief. Your subsequent actions with it should flow from what your inner spirit leads you to do.

Steven Farmer's *The Wounded Male* includes a powerful story of a thirty-eight-year-old man writing the following good-bye letter to his father:

Dear Dad,

I have to say good-bye, Dad. It seems strange to do so since you died so long ago. But I never got to say good-bye then. Why did you have to die? I was just getting to know you, and you went and died. It doesn't make any sense, but I'm really mad at you for doing so. I hated going to your funeral. You'll never know how much I cried afterward, all by myself. I couldn't let anybody else see me cry, because I had to be strong—just like you.

I didn't think you ever really knew me—your very own son. There were times when I hated you and times I admired you, and sometimes even I loved you.

Now it's time to say good-bye to you and let you go. It's scary to do this, but I must do it. I hate to leave you, but I must. Thanks for being my dad. You weren't always perfect, but you gave me a good start, and I'll always remember you.

Love,

Dale[9]

2. Creating memorials. Memorials have been used by the human race probably as long as we have been living. Rocks piled over a hastily dug grave, Plains Indian pole platforms, Civil War statues, huge and elaborate structures such as the Taj Mahal, Jewish Holocaust Museum, and others—we have always commemorated our losses and honored our griefs with something enduring and lasting. Something in the human psyche seems to demand the memorializing of significant events and griefs.

When I was a boy of about ten or eleven, I clearly remember the precision and care I took to bury a little bird I had accidentally killed by unwittingly bringing it into our house after it fell out of a nest. A scrawled epitaph on a piece of wood, "Dead because of a boy's foolishness," marked the hidden grave and somehow released the sadness and guilt I felt over my mistake.

There is room for much creativity, originality, and uniqueness in memorializing the griefs and losses of your life. Musically gifted people have written songs (Mike and the Mechanics, "The Living

Years"; Eric Clapton's "Tears in Heaven," in honor of his four-year-old son; Elton John's "The Man Who Never Died—Song for Guy"). Work-related projects have been dedicated to honoring grief (the 1991 Detroit Lions football season, leading to the NFL championship game, was dedicated to paralyzed lineman Mike Utley). Pictures can be framed and displayed, keepsake mementos ritually used and honored, personal projects undertaken, uniquely intimate rituals developed and performed regularly.[10]

In my own life, when my mentor, friend, and cousin, Fr. Louie Miller, died in November 1994, I found myself needing to create my own memorial to him. With the permission of his sister, I was able to obtain a uniquely intimate part of his life, sections of his personal journal entries up until five months before his death. After using these highly spiritual and insightful reflections as meditation material, I memorialized them by creating a carefully crafted, detailed memoir of Louie and his three priest brothers. Enclosed were pictures, news clippings, holy cards, letters, and Louie's own journal entries. This "Miller family album" (along with Louie's newly framed picture) have become priceless for me and have helped channel my grief, as well as honor my relatives' contribution to my life and ministry.

The mannequin used to teach CPR (named "Resusciannie") has a history connected to one man's griefquest. A grief-torn father invented Resusciannie after his daughter Annie drowned in a swimming pool because neither he nor anyone else knew how to do CPR to revive her. Annie's father memorialized the loss by his creative actions in griefquesting—he built Resusciannie to teach CPR nationwide. She is even dressed in the same red and blue outfit Annie died in as a reminder of how her death continues to bring forth new life.

---

3. Using Mother Nature's resources. For many men, the "great outdoors" has always had a special attraction. Many long-beloved male activities take place outdoors—sporting events, hunting, fishing, even auto repair and carpentry, and of course a whole range of exercise-related activities (hiking, jogging, skiing, and so on). Men should not neglect this area in finding creative activities to honor their griefquests.

Several men I know use gardening or yard work as healthy ways to make "earthy connections" with their grief. One man found that a four-day private backpacking trip enabled him to get past the male masks he'd been trained to wear, and to get in touch with the anger and hurt he felt over his recent sudden job loss. The tree-wounding ritual mentioned earlier could have contemporary applications and be used effectively today. Another man from Seattle honored his father's death by taking his ashes to the mountains he dearly loved to celebrate his father's own private funeral ceremony.[11]

In my life, I have heard many men testify freely to the restorative power of outdoor activities, when consciously connected with their inner griefs. Personally, I have always found that jogging or outdoor exercise has a tremendously calming and centering effect on my psyche, particularly when the griefs of life weigh me down. I have used outdoor exercise to deal with such personal griefs as Louie Miller's passing, vocational "necessary losses,"[12] and my mother's declining health. Through creative outdoor activity, I am able to release the negative grief energies of anger, frustration, or loneliness, as well as honor my losses.

4. Remembering and writing. Although writing is a more cerebral, logic-centered approach to dealing with grief (the opposite of the strong energies of emotion that grief generates), still it can be an effective way for some men to acknowledge and express their grief. The following reflection may help men get started here:

> Think back on the grief you have experienced or are experiencing . . . then write about it in as much detail as you are able. Remember specifics about the person, event, or loss. What was happening in your life at the time? How does this event or loss make you feel? Do you feel a gap in your being? How has the loss changed you? Have you shared the experience with anyone?

When I journal my thoughts about the pain of our problems to conceive a baby, I feel something released in me. I can't seem to talk about this stuff with anybody, even my wife. I guess I feel like I let her down somehow. But my journal has always been a haven for me. It's a place where I can write whatever comes along. . . . As I write, new doors open up in me. . . . Images and words and phrases and feelings come out—things I'm surprised are there inside of me. It has helped me talk with Wanda [my wife] about our problem more. . . .

5. Solitude and silence. We immediately tend to think of creative action as being noisy, loud, and energetic. However, the power of silence and solitude (much overlooked in our modern frenetic society) to touch a man's spirit and soul is awesome. Silence, if used correctly, can be as productive an action as physically engaging in some strenuous activity! Witness the following story from a man emerging from the grief of the breakup of a long, deeply emotional relationship:

> Jessie and I had been the best of friends, and had shared nearly everything for three years. The bond we had was deep and intimate . . . so the breakup was devastating. Though I sensed it coming, I think I still denied it. . . . Even after it was over, I couldn't handle the anger and loss. Then a friend let me use his cabin in northern Michigan for a week. . . . At first the silence and aloneness nearly killed me. But for the first time since the breakup, I had a chance to think about everything clearly, without distractions. I was surprised as heck to find that I could survive without her! I saw conflicts between us I'd never noticed before, or else I didn't want to see before. I realized how much of my life and energy she had consumed these past years, and how many of my own dreams I'd sacrificed.
>
> The ache and loneliness in me still was horrible, but by the end of the week it dawned on me that I COULD GO

ON! I didn't need her for my happiness. . . . I ended up burning many of her letters as my own farewell ceremony. Now, whenever I go back to John's cabin, I try to spend some time alone by myself. The solitude there always gets me in touch with what's most important in life. . . .

When you deal with people seriously ill, either yourself or others, try to honor the eloquence of God's silence. Babble if you must, but accept every invitation to desist. If the illness is your own, go for a walk, sit in a chapel, or just hold the loved ones you most cherish. If the illness is another's, listen for the time to stay silent, as well as the time to speak. There is a time to speak, but also a time to hold silence—to take it to your bosom like a love.
     John Carmody lecture entitled "A Theology of Illness"

---

6. Grief used as a catalyst into "new worlds." Since men tend toward action in healing their grief, it is not surprising that many men are able to allow their griefs to motivate them to new heights of insight, creativity, or inventiveness. The painfully different circumstances of grief often stimulate originality and creativity.

Charles Goodyear received a prison sentence resulting from a contempt of court citation. In prison, he became an assistant in the kitchen. While there, he allowed his anger and grief to stimulate several new ideas he had. As a result of this, Goodyear discovered a method for vulcanizing rubber, which has benefited all of us today in the form of better tires. Joe Scribben wrote "What a Friend We Have in Jesus" after mourning the loss of his young fiancée when her ship sank in a nearby bay. Young and athletic Harlan Sander's grief was having to stay home all day and cook for his brothers and sisters in Kentucky while his parents worked. He turned his grief into a blessing by becoming quite a good cook. You have no doubt eaten yourself at his "invention"—Kentucky Fried Chicken!

7. Other creative actions. Your own actions to honor grief and deal with the feelings within you can be as spontaneous and inventive as you want them to be. Use whatever talents and gifts you have—whether it be carpentry (a friend added a deck onto his house while processing his anger over being fired), sculpting (one man carved a bust of his deceased wife), music, painting, writing, or whatever. There are men who have created special Christmas cards to commemorate their wife's death. Some acknowledge painful transitions with a party or festive celebration.

As part of his griefquest in moving from Oklahoma to the pros, Dennis Byrd made himself a "memory bag" that he carried with him at every professional football game he ever played in. This leather pouch (given to him by his father) contained several personal items, as well as dirt from his Oklahoma home, which was ritually sprinkled on every field he played on. Robert Fulghum lays down on his grave plot from time to time; personally, I am content to visit our family plot in Michigan and stand silently next to my own future resting place.

[During my wife's dying] I used the Lutheran Book of Worship. I would sing the hymns of faith to her and in the midst of that would find the power reaching into my soul as well. I don't know if she heard the songs and the power of their words and tunes, but I know that I did.

Paul Thomton, *quoted by Herbert Anderson in* "The Gift of Grieving," The Lutheran, *February 1995*

I am sure I have omitted many other possible creative actions. A few more are listed in chapter twelve. I am always looking for new insights on how men can effectively deal with grief—so if you have an activity of your own, please let me know!

Notes

1. Thomas Golden's reflections were very insightful and helpful for this chapter. His wisdom from years of working with men in grief therapy can be found in three booklets he has written: *A Man's Grief: What Is Grief?*; *Different Paths Toward Healing*; and *Gender and Cultural Differences in Grief*. See appendix one for an ordering address.

2. Golden, *Different Paths Toward Healing*, pp. 31–32.

3. Ibid., p. 2.

4. Excerpts as submitted from *Rituals for Our Times*, by Evan Imber-Black and Janine Roberts, pp. 129–130. Copyright © 1993 by Evan Imber-Black and Janine Roberts. Reprinted by permission of HarperCollins Publishers.

5. Ibid., pp. 25–56.

6. We frequently and legitimately bemoan the fact that there are no rites of passage for our young people to mark their transition from childhood to adulthood. Unfortunately, however, too many young men (and women) today do indeed have informal "rites of passage"—into gang involvement, or marked by the beginning of alcohol or drug use. Healthier, more culturally appropriate rites are a desperate need.

7. Robert Fulghum, *From Beginning to End* (New York: Villard Publishing, 1995).

8. *Preparation*—planning the specifics of a ritual beforehand (perhaps including location, activity, inviting, time, and so on). *People*—Do you feel the need to do this activity by yourself? Will others be involved, or can you use a ritual already being done in your "family"? *Place*—The location of an action or ritual can have great significance. Is there an especially appropriate place or locale, with relevance either for you or connected with the loss? *Participation*—There are different levels of participation for any ritual. Will others be actively involved, or can they contribute something unique to this griefquest? Will children have any role? Would food or music or something else be necessary or helpful? *Presents*—Giving and receiving presents is integral in many rituals and relationships. Can your activity focus on some past "gift," present, or object that is part of your loss? Would gift-giving be in any way appropriate?

9. Steven Farmer, *The Wounded Male* (New York: Ballantine Books, 1991), pp. 41–42.

10. An interesting phenomenon has begun in recent years here in the United States, namely that of people spontaneously creating makeshift memorials at the site of tragedies. The killing of seven youths in Fox River Grove, Illinois, in an October 1995 bus-train accident gave

birth to an unofficial "shrine" at the site—consisting of rosaries, balloons, handwritten signs, poems, and symbols, such as a pack of chewing gum. The controversial discovery of the body of a murdered twelve-year-old girl in Cloverdale, California, led to a fifty-yard stretch of Highway 101 becoming a tourist attraction, with dozens of cars parked there at a time. In Chicago, names of young victims of violence are often spray painted on expressway overpasses.

Though some have called it morbid, this spontaneous new tradition (I don't recall anything like that happening in Dallas in 1963 after President Kennedy's shooting) is becoming a grief ritual. People continue to find ways to acknowledge and honor their griefs.

11. Golden, op. cit., p. 36.

12. As a committed Catholic priest, I long ago realized that for my own long-term mental and spiritual health, I had to mourn for the things I could and would not have by vocational choice. Specifically, of course, this includes a wife and committed marriage relationship, children of my own, grandchildren, and so on. It is a choice I now freely and happily make for the sake of the Kingdom and the spread of Jesus' Good News, but the "pearl" of my priesthood does have its price!

CHAPTER TEN

God and spirituality

Among all my patients in the second half of life (that is to say, over the age thirty-five), there has not been one whose problem in the last resort was not that of finding a religious outlook on life. It is safe to say that every one of them fell ill because he had lost that which the living religions of every age have given to their followers, and none of them has been really healed who did not regain his religious outlook.

Carl Jung, Modern Man in Search of a Soul

Joseph Bernardin—Cardinal Archbishop of Chicago

On 10 July 1982, the much-awaited announcement of the new archbishop of Chicago to succeed John Cardinal Cody was finally made in Rome. The man appointed for this great responsibility was Joseph Bernardin, then archbishop of Cincinnati, Ohio. From the very beginning, people in Chicago learned that Joseph Bernardin would be different than any who had preceded him in that position. His frequent letters and correspondence with archdiocesan priests were signed simply "Joseph, your brother." People in Chicago came to know and love him as a gentle, spiritual man, ready to face any hard decisions, but always humble, diplomatic, warm, and pastoral. In just ten years, our brother Joseph became a well-known, much-respected, and comforting figure in all the avenues and alleys, subways and suburbs of the Windy City.

But as we all know, no man on this earth (no matter how famous or prestigious) is free from grief, struggle, and pain. "Joe" Bernardin, Archbishop of Chicago, was no exception. In November 1993, a false charge of sexual impropriety was brought against him by a young man from Cincinnati, Steven Cook, who also filed a ten-million-dollar lawsuit against him personally. Though all charges against Cardinal Bernardin were dismissed at his accuser's request in February 1994 (and a powerful, "grace-filled" meeting with Steven Cook occurred one month later), a mere six months later, a second grief stunned the cardinal. In June 1995, Joe Bernardin was diagnosed with pancreatic cancer. Thus, the man who only a year before had dedicated a shrine to Saint Peregrine (the patron of those with cancer) at a local basilica, now himself had to undergo twenty-eight days of intense radiation and chemotherapy treatments, followed by a two-year maintenance therapy program of weekly injections. Cardinal Bernardin died of this cancer in November 1996, but in the interim, he continued to walk day by day in hope and healing, giving immense hope, faith, and love to all who knew and respected him.

Most people by now have heard the well-publicized facts of our brother Joseph's story. What they most likely have *not* heard are the struggles, feelings, and personal grief of the man *behind* the story. We are privileged to have the cardinal share his own personal reflections on these two well-publicized griefs.

Our brother Joseph: "Two traumatic events . . ."

During the past two years, I have faced two traumatic events that have profoundly impacted my life and ministry. The first was an accusation that, some seventeen years ago, while I was Archbishop of Cincinnati, I had sexually abused a college seminarian by the name of Steven Cook. While I knew the accusation was false, within hours it became a cause célèbre not only in the United States but also around the world. News of the accusation was leaked to the press one day before the suit was filed in Cincinnati. As I learned about the accusation, media representatives in Chicago began gathering outside the Archdiocesan Pastoral Center and my residence. For the next ten or twelve days, I was constantly confronted by the media. I made myself completely available to them and declared my innocence, but I was totally humiliated and embarrassed. CNN, which had prior knowledge of what was going to happen, aired a program in which I was depicted as having "fallen from grace."

The second event occurred when I learned that I had a malignant pancreatic tumor, one of the most aggressive forms of cancer. This took me completely by surprise because I had no symptoms of such a malignancy. Within days I had to undergo radical surgery (known as the Whipple procedure). Suddenly, for the first time in my life, I had to face directly the prospect of a premature death. In one brief moment, all my plans for the future had to be put on hold; everything in my personal and ministerial life had to be re-evaluated from a new perspective.

"You wonder if you're dreaming . . ."

Confronting malignant cancer is hard enough for any person, but to have this follow on the heels of false sexual allegations—this is a heavy burden indeed to have to carry. For Joseph, it was no different. He wrestled with the hurt and negative emotions of these two stunning crises. Simply because he was the cardinal of the second largest archdiocese in the United States did not mean he was immune from the pain of grief. Cardinal Bernardin reflects here on the painful ramifications of these sudden events on his faith and life:

> Several years ago, in a conversation I had with several priests, I was asked what were my two greatest fears. Without much reflection, I told them that I had always had two fears: one was being accused of anything serious; the other was being afflicted with an aggressive type of cancer. Within two years, both occurred!

The false accusation suddenly put my ministry in jeopardy. Even though I knew I was innocent, I did not know what people would think and how my ministry might be undermined. Even some people who believed in my innocence said (and wrote) that, whatever the outcome, I would be "damaged." Emotionally, I experienced at times a certain anxiety, a certain fear. I would wake up at night wondering, if the case went to trial, whether the jurors would believe me!

The unexpected news that I had an aggressive form of cancer bewildered me. As a matter of fact, I initially had difficulty believing that the diagnosis was correct. I felt very vulnerable. . . . Watching the news, it was hard to believe it was me they were talking about. I'd see all these charts, my insides up there. [The reporters] would ask about chances of my survival! It was kind of a feeling where you wonder if you're dreaming. . . .

In my convalescence after the surgery . . . I would find myself weeping at times (something I seldom did before). Upon reflection, I discovered that the cause was a fear of the return of the cancer, or the fear that my recovery would not be complete and thus my ministry would be affected, or a concern about the future of my mother who is nearly ninety-one years old and in a nursing home. But these reactions are part of the human condition . . . so I have made no effort to hide or deny them. The important thing is how we handle them. . . .

There's no contradiction at having fear or being emotionally distraught at times and at the same time being a person of faith. I know we're on the road to something better. But to say that you have no fear, no anxiety—I think that is somewhat abnormal. . . .

"It was my faith that made it possible to cope . . ."

For the clergy of the world, grief presents a special challenge. In one way, we priests and ministers are more equipped to deal with personal loss because we (by our vocation) confront sin, sickness, weakness, death, and loss on a routine basis. But in another way, we clergy can easily become immune to our own pain and inner emotions. We who try to give hope to others often do not know how to give to ourselves. Joe Bernardin, however, is a man who knew where to go for comfort, and he slowly learned how to cope with his grief:

> It was my faith that made it possible for me to cope positively with these two events. For forty-three years as a priest and twenty-nine as a bishop, I have counseled people to trust in the Lord, to believe that he would give them strength. . . . But when I faced the traumas myself, I discovered that I truly believed it; that it was, indeed, part of my very being! My faith gave me a perspective, a peace, a hope that enabled me to deal positively with the realities I was facing. I literally felt the presence of the Lord; it was as if he was saying to me: "I will not abandon you. I will walk with you and help you through all of this." When I told this to the media . . . some of them had a hard time understanding what I meant.
>
> Even though . . . my faith sustained me [and] I never felt closer to the Lord, . . . in the first weeks after the surgery, I found it difficult, indeed almost impossible, to pray in the way to which I was accustomed. I said to many friends, "You had better pray when you are well, because you may not be able to do so when you are seriously ill." [This] inability to engage in the more formal prayers, though, in no way proved to be an obstacle to the Lord's presence.
>
> In addition to my faith, I was blessed by the support, love, and prayers of so many people. When the accusation was made, I received countless letters from people who said they believed in my innocence and were praying for me. Their support was a great blessing.
>
> . . . When it was announced that I had pancreatic cancer, I received nearly 12,000 letters and cards. In addition, I received phone calls from Pope John Paul II, President Bill Clinton, and Mother Teresa of Calcutta. The support and

prayers of so many people gave me encouragement; they bolstered my faith.

Somehow, with God's grace and the prayers and support of many people, I was able to move beyond the fear; I was able to put aside the non-important, non-essential things that so often hold us hostage. I was able to see things in a new perspective. Suddenly, the difference between the important things and the non-important things came more sharply into focus. Certainly when you come face-to-face with death as I have, it changes your view of everything. . . .

"I had a credibility I didn't have before . . ."

Finally, in 1996, I asked Joe Bernardin if he could share with us some of the wisdom he learned from his two recent grief experiences. He shared these insights that he had learned and that he hoped to take with him for the rest of his journey through life:

> Traumas of this kind change your perspective. You begin to realize that so much of your time and effort has been devoted to what is not important! I intend to spend more time on what truly benefits people, both personally and communally, and less time on petty squabbles and bureaucratic red tape, which do not contribute very much to the individual or common good. I know that good order is needed, as are sound policies whose formulation requires much time and effort. Moreover, I do not intend to abdicate my responsibilities as archbishop. But I will exercise more discretion as to where I will focus my time and attention. Something like this also brings you to the realization that you don't have to keep running all the time. I don't intend to fade from sight. I don't intend to retire. But I do intend to do the best I can during the day and try to be satisfied. And that's all I can do!
>
> Second, I have learned that you should use your experience to help others who are undergoing the same difficulties.

I have become an "unofficial chaplain" of cancer patients in the Chicago area. During the weeks of radiation and chemotherapy, I met many other cancer patients. Somehow now I had a credibility I didn't have before. They and I have been helped by our praying together, sharing our experiences, and encouraging each other. Somehow, a prayer or blessing from someone who "knows" means more. Now I receive daily requests, either by mail or phone, to write notes or make calls to other cancer patients, assuring them of my prayers and support.

Finally . . . one thing has become very clear. The basic message is that people do not want priests or bishops who have political savvy. They do not want good managers (though they will complain if you do not manage well!). They do not expect us to be "fixers" or to have the solution for every problem. No, they want holy men. They want us to be signs of God's presence, a sign of hope. This has made a profound impact on me. . . . This is a message I will not forget in the future, and it is one I will share with my priests.

"Morals" for modern men

GOD. The word itself is powerful. It is a word guaranteed to draw some reaction from anyone at any place in the world. *God. Yahweh. Allah. Jehovah.* Every culture that ever existed has had some concept of a supreme being with influence and power on this earth. Every culture somehow deals with death and tragedy in a philosophy of life that arises from its unique approach to the Divine.[1] But only Christianity has as its very foundation a mind-boggling religious paradox—a God who himself died in order to give eternal purpose and meaning to our deaths and losses.

Jesus Christ, the Son of God, chose to connect himself with grief, loss, and *all* human experiences in an intimate and eternal way. He knew grief and loss himself because he risked becoming human, having real feelings and friendships.[2] His death and Resurrection pushed the envelope of consciousness past sorrow and loss to a broader purpose and meaning. Developing an understanding of and relationship with this God is what we have come to call *spirituality*. Spirituality and faith (that is, having a personal and active relationship with the Supreme Being) is what ultimately provides the *single greatest source of healing, strength, and hope for any man struggling with grief and loss*.

God, grant me serenity to accept the things I cannot change; courage to change the things I can; and wisdom to know the difference.

Reinhold Neibuhr, The Serenity Prayer

A personal faith life gives grief perspective

No man on the face of this earth is immune from grief and pain— not even the spiritual leader of millions of Chicago Catholics. Joe Bernardin's story is a powerful proof of this, but it is also a dynamic lesson in the value of a personal faith life (not just organized religion) for handling our griefs. When a man has a deep personal bond with his God, takes time to nourish it with prayer and meditation, and acts upon his faith foundations with integrity —he possesses a balance, a perspective, an energy source that will uphold him through the most severe personal storms. A personal faith life (a life of the soul) gives a man perspective, grounding, roots, and balance in the face of life's uncertainties.

At times of pain and loss, people often confuse *faith* and *religion*. Religion has to do with organizing and structuring the experience of the Divine in life. Many men today do not profess a close bond with religion in their life, for a variety of reasons (hypocrisy, irrelevance, sign of "weakness," past hurts, disinterest, sheer boredom). While ritualizing faith is beneficial for comprehending the Incomprehensible and Unknowable One, we should also realize its shortcomings and limitations. Organized religion, by definition, can provide a comforting and healing structure for a man in times of grief, but we should not expect it to provide "answers" for the pain of grief. Religion is only a tool (a valuable one) to help structure what only a man's *personal faith* can reveal to him.[3]

Faith by definition is belief, trust, and a certain dependence upon a Power and Being beyond ourselves. Faith pulls a man out of his own small little world and opens him up to a bigger Reality. Tragedy, loss, death, or grief tends to pull a man *within himself* as he obsesses over, mourns, and grieves his loss. But when a man accepts God as a personally meaningful and central force in his life (a decision that may have to be repeated often in life), that man anchors himself to an unchanging Truth, a "Rock of Ages" that not only holds him securely but also transforms the meaning and interpretation of every event in life. In times of grief and loss, men need to know that, despite what they feel at the moment, there is still meaning and hope and value in the world. There is a Love, a Power bigger than them who carries them gently in their inability to even walk on their own.

Joe Bernardin was certainly a religious man, being the archbishop of Chicago, but in his grief, it was not so much his religion as his immense personal faith that held him fast. Cardinal Bernardin believed that God indeed is real—the Lord is present even when not seen and is powerful even in human confusion. (Hebrews 11:1: "Now faith is the assurance of things hoped for, the conviction of things not seen.")

It was my faith that made it possible for me to cope with these two events. For forty-three years, I have counseled people to trust in the Lord . . . but when I faced the traumas myself, I discovered that I truly believed it. . . . My faith gave me a perspective, a peace, a hope that enabled me to deal positively with the realities I was facing.

It was as if God was saying, "I will not abandon you. I will walk with you and help you through all of this. . . ."

Cardinal Joseph Bernardin

When grief shakes our faith and values: Linus's story

Why? The question may stick in the mouth of one who is griev-ing. The emotional impact of a job loss, death, personal problem, or whatever, sends a man into a whirlpool of emptiness, loneliness, and confusion. Some look to the heavens and conclude that God must be detached, uncaring, and impersonal in enacting his divine will, and that he may even be a "cosmic sadist," playing games with his subjects as one might toy with the pieces on a chess-board. Even a man who has had a long-term relationship with God may find his God strangely quiet and ominously distant when the blanket of sorrow descends upon him.

Linus is a man in his late forties, happily married with chil-dren, successful in his chosen field of editorial work for a large company. His faith has always been important to him and his fam-ily, but the griefs of his life severely shook that faith. He and his wife suffered three miscarriages early in their marriage, the final one occurring just two months before his father died. He talks freely now about the struggle with God and with himself that these events triggered:

> Each miscarriage was worse than the one before. I truly felt abandoned—even betrayed—by God. [With the last miscar-riage] I knew my father was dying (advanced cancer), and yet my wife was pregnant, and we took this as sort of a "con-solation prize" from God. Yes, we were going to lose a much-loved father at age seventy, but we were going to gain a much-longed-for child. Isn't that the way God worked?
>
> . . . The idea of an "eye for an eye"—I think I got to believing that God operated that way. When we were good, we got good little rewards—from our parents—and from God. Basically I was/am from a good family. We did all the right things, and yet my totally innocent father suffered cru-elly and long with cancer. It made no sense to me to be pray-ing and not have our prayers answered. I stewed and stormed and protested and cried—all very silently . . . like a good

man. Instead of mourning like a human, I mourned like a
man . . . like my dad had taught me to mourn when he
and my mother suffered their own miscarriages: you hold it
in, you try to "forget about it," and you go on. I was angry
and felt abandoned by God.

There are no easy answers nor swift resolution for griefs like
this. Yes, God is very real. He loves us as his own precious posses-
sions and hears our prayers. That is fact and truth. But, yes, three
miscarriages and losing his father hurt like hell for Linus, and
there was nothing that could take away that human ache and loss.
These two realities—one so comforting, the other so shocking—
may have to exist side by side for a while. Being shaken by grief
does not mean one has to abandon belief in an apparently "cruel"
God, nor does it mean that one should deny the overwhelming
emotions that temporarily wash over us. God remains with us in
these dark places and valleys, even when we feel out of control,
lost, and angry.

Still, that's what we're all asked to do: to believe perseveringly in
the dark in something we once saw in the light, to believe stead-
fastly in something that once appeared evident in joy.
                              Louis Evely, That Man Is You

Grief most often *will* shake a man to his core, as it did for
Linus. But a life and faith shaken up is not always a bad thing.
Though there may never be human reasons sufficient enough to
"explain" miscarriages or deaths or broken relationships, our God
can use all events and incidents that occur and blend them
smoothly yet mysteriously into the variegated, multi-threaded ta-
pestry of his strange and unexplainable plan. For Linus, his grief
and "abandonment" became a necessary wound, eventually used to
push his faith deeper, beyond the "immature" first stages of trust
("If I'm good, God will give me good things") to the deeper, more
mature stages of faith. It led him to a necessary grief-question.

Is your God too small?

One of our biggest problems with God is that we consistently sell God short. As humans, we tend to unconsciously impose our logic and limitations on God, and try to force God into nice, manageable niches in our mind. However, God's ways are not our ways (as Isaiah 55:8–9 tells us): "For as the heavens are higher than the earth, so are my ways higher than your ways." Thus, an utterly essential question every person needs to ask himself is, *Is my God too small?* In other words, are my old ideas, images, and concepts of God too outdated, immature, or untested to be relied upon in present moments of stress or grief?

At times of grief, men urgently need to change, review, or renew their concept of God. What has been your own level of faith or belief in God? Every man who has shared his story in this book has wrestled with God's relevance and place in his life as he struggled with these issues:

♦ **Is your concept of God "too small" and outdated?** For example, believing that God shouldn't allow any bad things to occur; that he is judgmental, severe, distant, strict, unreachable, or uncaring. The God revealed in the Scriptures, Jesus Christ, cried and grieved over the death of his good friend Lazarus. He was humanly and emotionally terrified to the point of sweating blood (a proven medical possibility in severe stress). This God cries and mourns our losses—for he has walked this same road before us, struggled with the same demons, and knows well our weaknesses.

This is the true God as he revealed himself—not demanding, threatening, or intimidating, but affirming, supporting, encouraging . . . a gentle God who invites us to trust and believe that he offers a better way of living.

♦ **Is God a priority in life?** If God has not been, you might ask yourself why not, and re-examine the evidence for God. Note the positive impact faith has had on people you know. Any man drowning in a pool would be foolish indeed to ignore a lifeline, a Source of hope and peace that has rescued millions before him.

◆ **Has faith already been a part of your life?** If your faith has been important to you, spend time "wrestling" with God, allowing him to walk with you through your sorrows. Do not cease praying, even though it may seem barren, dry, and useless. Read Scripture passages that relate to your present feelings, and allow yourself to enter into them without expecting easy answers.

Linus himself, like Jacob (Genesis 32:22–32) and Job before him, wrestled with God and found himself changing, expanding to take on a new concept of God, and thus a renewed spirituality and faith life:

> . . . What helped was doing a lot of reading, praying, and listening to people who said what happened might have had a higher purpose, but wasn't something God wanted—especially the suffering. "We simply can't believe that God wants only our good. God cries with us." These were the words and ideas that brought new understandings. It also helped for me to read these words: "If logic tells you there is no [loving] God, don't give up on God, give up on logic." I needed to see that just because it would have made good logical sense for God to give us this child instead of a miscarriage, this didn't mean it was time to give up on God.
>
> So, instead of looking for a God of power and might who would "fix" things, I started looking for a God of love and consolation who would really fix things. The answer time has shown me . . . is that God answers prayers in God's way, not our way, and in God's time frame, not ours. This revelation came through loud and clear in time: Our God is a God of love and care and comfort and compassion, not only a "John Wayne" God of power and might who comes to our rescue at the big shootout.
>
> [Now] I try not to separate God from real life. We can't keep God in a drawer that we pull out on Sunday mornings or on the battlefield or at the hour of our death. Our God is near when we're changing jobs, and when we're changing tires, and when we're changing diapers.

Beneath and above the shifting sands of time, the uncertainties that darken our day, and the vicissitudes that cloud our nights is a wise and loving God. The universe is not a tragic expression of meaningless chaos but a marvelous display of orderly cosmos. . . . Man is not a wisp of smoke from a limitless smoldering but a child of God created "a little lower than the angels." Above the manyness of time stands the one eternal God, with wisdom to guide us, strength to protect us, and love to keep us. His boundless love supports and contains us as a mighty ocean contains and supports the tiny drops of every wave.

Martin Luther King, The Strength to Love

Griefquesting in a faith-filled way— What can men do?

[For men or women in deep pain, grief, or depression:]

1. Spend some time reading and reflecting on the "Cardinal Rules of Crisis" (appendix two). These eight brief rules will help you discover an immediate sense of balance or priority at times when everything around you seems to be crumbling.

2. Take time to re-evaluate your concepts of God, and to renew your life of the soul, your personal faith relationship with God. Reflect on the questions and comments listed on the page before this one. . . . Allow yourself to "wrestle" with God, to have God enter into your pain and walk with you, side by side, to a more peaceful place.

3. Learn how to pray, or else rediscover prayer in a new way. First Thessalonians 5:17–18 says, "Pray without ceasing, give thanks in all circumstances; for this is the will of God in Christ Jesus for you." If you do not have a regular habit of daily prayer, begin by setting aside a definite time each day for God. In other words, make an appointment with God (in your calendar, if need be) each day. Then read the section in chapter twelve on "Developing a daily prayer life."

If prayer has been part of your regular routine, realize that it may take on a different style or pattern now. Be willing to simply sit quietly before God, to seek without expecting answers. Maintaining a prayer ritual may be extremely helpful—whether in regular worship at your church, Scripture reading, or some other structured prayer form. Simple prayer, without many words at all (perhaps repeating a word or phrase over and over meditatively), may be especially calming.

4. Sit through your dark times with patience and trust, knowing that "there's gotta be a morning after." The most basic Christian virtue of all, the defining edge of a man's faith, is hope. These words from my old college spiritual director contain much consolation for those struggling in faith: "I get my encouragement and hope from two sources: the pledge of the Master himself, and my knowledge of the history of the people of God, the knowledge that we have passed through times infinitely worse than this and survived."

Everywhere around the world, at this moment, a billion men are seeking their God, fasting for visions, expiating their sins, singing divine praises, and enduring hardships for faith and justice. Men are naturally deeply religious, all right; it is just that our modern culture provides little help for them.
Patrick Arnold, SJ, America magazine, 7 October 1989

Notes

1. In a *New York Times* book review in the early 1990s, M. G. Michaelson wrote that virtually everyone who has seriously studied the subject of dying has come out of it believing in some form of life after death. Elisabeth Kübler-Ross, the author of the famed *Death and Dying*, is such an example. She did not believe in life after death until she started working with dying patients. Now she believes "beyond the shadow of a doubt."

2. Hebrews 4:15: "For we do not have a high priest who is unable to sympathize with our weaknesses, but we have one who in every respect has been tested as we are, yet without sin. Let us therefore approach the throne of grace with boldness, so that we may receive mercy and find grace to help in time of need."

3. An interesting study done in 1995 by sociologists Robert Duff and Lawrence Hong studied 700 residents of six retirement communities along the West Coast of the United States. In this study, they discovered that anxiety about death is reduced significantly when the elderly participate in religious rituals. Some comments from this study: "Frequency of attending religious services is significantly associated with low death anxiety." "Rituals create both a sense of belonging and a sense of transcendence. Rituals are the key. Rituals are a glue that bind us together. We remember those who've passed on and the religious acts we shared with them." The study found that communities with the highest rates of participation in religious services showed the lowest death anxiety. The study is entitled "Age Density, Religiosity, and Death Anxiety in Retirement Communities," and is published in the September 1995 issue of *Review of Religious Research*.

CHAPTER ELEVEN

Personal honesty, awareness, and integrity

Louie Miller (1913–94): "A wise man teaches me the way . . ."

Fr. Louis Miller, CSSR, was many things to me. He was a brother priest, a cousin and family member, a friend and fellow worker, a Socrates to my Plato. I suppose he would be surprised to hear himself described this way by me, for (in typically male fashion) I never quite got around to letting him know how powerful a role he played for me. It wasn't until his death in the fall of 1994 that I became fully aware of the impact of his life on mine. Now I realize how his "wiseman energy" can be a guide for all of us men today.

Background

Louie and my own father (Robert Miller, as well) grew up playing together as cousins in Grand Rapids, Michigan, in the early 1900s. They were about the same age and became close friends, a bond that remained strong until my dad's death in 1967. Louie's three brothers had already entered the seminary of the Redemptorist Order, and his parents, Wenzl and Margaret, hesitated to allow Louie to go when he wanted to follow his brothers' footsteps. After several years they relented, seeing his strong commitment and vocation. (Perhaps also because they had grown tired of Louie cutting holes in newspapers to create a vestment and play "priest" in his room!)

Twelve years later, in June 1939, Louie was ordained a Redemptorist priest. He spent his first years teaching in the seminary, studying journalism, and helping with a then-fledgling magazine entitled *Liguorian*. As World War II came around, Louie enlisted as a chaplain, serving in New Guinea and the Philippines. Later he was recalled to service for the Korean War. His postwar career then began. For twenty-nine years he lived in Liguori, Missouri, helping found a publishing company there, as well as writing for the burgeoning new ministry of pamphlets and the *Liguorian* magazine. Following his brother Don's footsteps, Louie became editor of the magazine in 1961.

His writing style was marked by forthright honesty, deep faith, and a great balance between all points of view. He wrote during the turbulent 60s, and was not afraid to take well-thought-out social stands on the issues of the day. Louie's editorial on Martin Luther King Jr. after his assassination was some of his best writing. Typically, his social and spiritual balance in the article resulted in a number of subscription cancellations. Louie commented, "I suppose the cancellations could be prevented if one never took a stand or made a forceful statement, but this is no time to remain neutral and colorless in the face of the vexing problems that our Church and country face."

Some (especially today) may wonder about a priest's commitment or motivation, especially as clergy numbers decline, but Louie's own beliefs never wavered. In one Liguorian *article, he writes: "I believe that . . . I can, by the grace of God, serve as a source of guidance and encouragement and warning to God's people. . . . I cherish the humble hope that my manner of life will remind others of life's spiritual dimension."*

Mentor for my masculine maturity

In the last fifteen years of his life, Louie's and my paths began to cross often. In 1977, Louie had moved on to doing retreat work in Illinois, followed later by involvement with Marriage Encounter, parish ministry, peace and justice work, and a host of other activities. His retirement years were never quiet, inactive, or dull! As we worked together on a number of preached parish missions, I grew closer to this man whom I perceived to be aging so gracefully and wisely. Here was a man of balance, faith, wisdom, and integrity—not a "traditional" priest, distant and removed, but a normal man struggling to be faithful, honest to his call, and close to his God. I instinctively sensed that this wise man had much to teach me, a young man ordained nearly forty years after him.

My own father had died in 1967, and I know now that Louie became for me more than merely a father figure; he also became a role model, a mentor, a guide to masculine maturity. As I struggled through the various crises of my own early priesthood, Louie was a stabilizing, compassionate force for me.

A quote from his journal (kept faithfully throughout his life) offers an insight into what he perhaps subconsciously recognized as his role for me and others: "Could it be the special task of the old to bear living witness to youth against fear of death, whether great or slight? Reconciled to life, reconciled to the earth . . . old age [is] less the 'harvest of life' as [it is] the commission to draw back the curtain slowly from the threshold of new life."

A rare man of integrity

In reflecting on Louie's life, what strikes me the most is that he was a man of tremendous balance and integrity. Whereas many men wear different masks in their public or private lives, Louie did not. He was not "two people"—what you saw in public was how he was in private. A longtime friend traveled with him to Disney World and noted that Louie relished the spectacular sights there by day, yet at night never failed to first read his office, then another book, and finally to kneel at his bedside to say night prayers. Louie's values and beliefs were soft-spoken but consistent. He had balance between the spiritual and material worlds, between theory and action, between laughter and seriousness. Louie lived privately what he preached and spoke about publicly. There was no duplicity or subterfuge anywhere in his being.

Father Louie was a man who continued to learn and grow as he aged. This is one of the most amazing and rare gifts any man can have. Many people reach a point in life where they become hardened, or settle into an often stagnant, rigid worldview based on visions of past glories. Not so with Louie! He was always expanding his mind with books (he read at least fifty books a year for most of his life), workshops, lectures, and challenging new ideas. For example, late in life Louie became deeply involved with peace and justice issues. He not only gave talks and led prayer services, but he also sat on diocesan commissions and even traveled to poor countries like El Salvador to raise money to buy cows for the villages! The story is told that the people of a village there called Guarjila finally said, "Stop! No more cows! Now we need chickens, school buildings, and health clinics." So Louie willingly took on these new causes.

A woman in Louie's Matisse, Missouri, parish recalls a parish retreat she attended with him: "I'd been a Catholic for only two years; I was still uncomfortable around priests. I figured Father Louie just came along to celebrate Mass. I was wrong! I can still see him participating in the 'trust-building exercise' at our 1987 retreat. He stood on a platform about ten feet off the ground and fell backward into the waiting arms of eight people. He was seventy-four years old at the time!"

Louie's griefquest—Approaching his last days

In the last years of his life, Louie was very aware at all times of what lay ahead. Even though he was still quite healthy, Louie seemed to have a deep inner sense that death would soon be coming for him. As was his style, he confronted it honestly, bluntly, realistically, and without fear.

On August 28, 1993, Louie wrote in his journal:

Thanks be to God for the gift of peace in these later years! Not even any great apprehension of death, though at the age of eighty I have to suppose that the angel of death may be waiting for me at the next turn of the road. My only apprehension is the sickness and pain that may precede death. But whatever comes—let it come! My trust is in the name of the Lord!

In April 1994, seven months before his death, Louie wrote:

The shadow of death hangs over me. . . . Premonitions abound, for her [his sister, Mary, in the hospital] and for myself (unexpected weaknesses—angina?), but which are true and which are false? The deep mystery of our crossover moment. What awaits us on the other side of the boundary? Stepping over it is such a unique and personal experience—not to be shared with anyone!

Finally, on the day of his last earthly birthday, April 11, 1994, Father Louie wrote but twelve words in his journal. How beautifully they sum up the passion and peace, the insight and integrity by which he lived his life: "Eighty-one years old! How close is the finish line?" He concluded with the three words that close nearly every journal entry. Fitting words for a man of God whose faith nourished so many: "COME, LORD JESUS!" Louis Gerard Miller passed away suddenly on November 19, 1994, after heart surgery four days earlier.

My first cold in years has settled in . . . another token of mortality, of the vulnerability of our physical envelope, and a call to be prepared for the final outbreak of my human fragility.

Thanks be to God I am at peace in this waning time, even a little anxious to depart and put behind me the frustrations, misjudgments, and misunderstandings of life, the chaotic mess which we humans have gotten ourselves into. I am ready, Lord! Come, Lord Jesus!

From Louie's journal, several months before his death

"Morals" for modern men

The word *integrity* has lost its meaning in today's world. The dictionary defines *integrity* as "adherence to a code of values; utter sincerity, honesty, and candor." But in a world where the bottom line and even greed are corporate norms, where corruption at all levels of government is common, and where "Do your own thing" has become the ultimate ethical guideline, one can easily wonder where men of integrity have gone today.

Integrity comes from the Latin word *integritas*, meaning "completeness" or "unity." The word denotes soundness, completeness, or unity in a person, being able to hold all aspects of human life and divine (eternal) reality in balance within oneself. Far too few men today strive for this integrity and balance in every aspect of their life. This is an underlying reason why many of us find the griefs and problems of this world so shattering and overwhelming. Literally, we are "out of balance," and we lack the attitudinal resources to adequately cope.

How much integrity a man strives for (namely, how he tries to balance ethical values, personal life priorities, emotions, outer commitments, and inner work) has a great effect on his capacity to grieve losses in a healthy way. No man can ever properly prepare for grief and loss, nor can he escape the pain and turmoil it brings. But healthy, balanced foundational attitudes and values can better equip a man to deal effectively with the griefs and loss-es that come his way in the normal course of life. They are not as likely to have as shattering an effect upon him as they tend to have in men who are out of balance with life and disconnected within.

Small is the number of them that see with their own eyes, and feel with their own hearts.

Albert Einstein

Learning some foundational attitudes

Louie Miller is a rare but precious example of a balanced man of integrity in today's world. Certainly he was not perfect, nor would he have ever claimed to be (his journal reflects the self-doubts and uncertainties that marked his humanness). But the overall balance and integrity he showed in his words and actions is an example for all men to strive for. When those "dark hours" of life do hap-pen and a man must walk through grief, he will be much better equipped if he has already established solid foundational attitudes.

From all the men witnessing in this book, we can learn sev-eral principles that can help a man build solid personal founda-tions for an effective griefquest. It is much like laying or pouring a proper foundation for a new house. Once the "below ground" basics are in place, construction can go on without major dilem-mas, despite problems. First, let us outline several problem areas men need to confront honestly in themselves. These are the bar-riers, or "foundational faults," which can sabotage our griefquests.

1. Imbalanced life priorities—when a man's values are out of order. There is often a lack of harmony or balance between the aspects of life that nourish the human spirit of a man and those that erode or even destroy that spirit. Leaving aside more obvious examples such as substance abuse, criminal activity, or marital infidelity, there are other values that are not bad in themselves but are potentially destructive if they have excessive importance in life. The classic examples for any man would be money, success, power, sexuality, and work.

A man's job and career, for example, can become a dominating and even harmful influence in life if not kept in proper perspective. Perhaps because of our intrinsically autonomous and independent nature, a man needs to have work or a career—it is essential for a healthy sense of masculine identity.

But when working (or any other above-mentioned value) becomes excessive or even compulsive, a certain flatness, dryness, and narrowness can infect a man's life. He lacks contact with the life-giving and spirit-nourishing aspects of life, and sets himself up to fall when crisis rocks his nice but falsely ordered world.

2. Living an unaware life—going through life with little self-consciousness or inner work. The majority of men, and perhaps the entire world, go through life with little deeper consciousness than what their next meal will be or what they'll do on their upcoming day off. People tend to be afraid to ask the hard questions of life. The book *Finding Your Place in the Universe* phrases it well: "The really dangerous words may be . . . three-letter words: . . . words like 'why'—the question that disturbs and upsets our quiet complacency. 'Why' is the hard question we often dread to ask. . . . Why do I do the things that I do? Why am I afraid to ask the hard questions that may challenge my comfortable life?"[1]

The unexamined life is no life.
Socrates (as quoted in Louie Miller's journal)

---

3. A nonrelational lifestyle—avoiding commitments, or running from them. Especially in the past several decades, many young men seem to have great difficulty making personal commitments. But older men as well, even those married or already "committed" to someone, can have essentially the identical problem.

Because men tend not to be relational by nature, we often find it discomforting and difficult to enter into and maintain personal and intimate (not necessarily sexual) relationships with either women or men.[2] Thus, a true danger for men is that we can become indifferent and dispassionate in relationships, to the point of "using" people (both men and women in intimate or business relationships) purely for our own independent purposes.

The songwriter B. J. Thomas sang it well long ago: "Loving things and using people only leads to misery. . . . Using things and loving people—that's the way it ought to be." Even as a priest, and unmarried by vowed choice, Louie Miller had close and dear friends whom he allowed to deeply affect his life. His funeral Mass was jammed with people who shared freely about the intimate and deep effect his life and words had on their marriage and families.

The most important human endeavor is the striving for morality in our actions. Our inner balance and even our integrity depend on it. Only morality in our actions can give beauty and dignity to life.
Albert Einstein

Cultivating an attitude of integrity

On the positive side of the spectrum, there are several attitudes men should actively work to cultivate. These are the positive foundation stones or building blocks that underlie a healthy, balanced, enlightened masculine identity. The great men of the world—men like King, Gandhi, Churchill, Edison, Lincoln, and others—all built their greatness upon attitudes such as these. Perhaps that is why they were able to pass through the griefs of their own lives and make such significant contributions to our world.

1. A sense of order and priority in life. A man establishes healthy, balanced priorities for the activities and commitments of his life, and he lives life in an ordered, balanced fashion.

If a man wants to be successful in life, the most essential question he should ask himself is, "What are you going to live your life for?" What is to be your motivation, your inspiration, your driving force for living and acting? Jesus Christ says it so well: "For where your treasure is, there your heart will be also" (Luke 12:34). The greatest men have been men who lived with a sense of purpose, direction, values, perspective, and order to their lives.

A man who lives for narrow, self-gratifying values may find those needs fulfilled—only to discover a gap in his soul, an existential uneasiness. Only when we live for something other than ourselves—for an Other that gives direction and purpose to life, for others we love, for others in need, or for causes bigger than self—only then will happiness come. Again, Jesus says it best, "Strive first for the kingdom of God and his righteousness, and all these things will be given to you as well" (Matthew 6:33).

Right now, put this book down, and take out a blank sheet of paper. Put down numbers from 1 to 5. Then pause for a moment and write down the top five concerns and worries of your life right now. After you are done, examine and reflect on this list. If there is a preponderance of self-centered concerns, and a dearth of values such as family, God, community outreach—then perhaps you need to seriously re-evaluate your life priorities. Getting one's priorities in order is like pointing your car in the right direction—it may not *take* you there, but inevitably it *will lead* there.

I do not know how your lives will be, but this much I do know: The only ones among you who will truly be happy are those who seek and find how to serve.

Commencement address by Dr. Albert Schweitzer

A man is only as good as what he loves.

Saul Bellow, Nobel Prize–winning author

---

2. Integrity in living a life of values and ethics at work, home, and elsewhere. The vital role of ethics, morality, and personal conscience has almost disappeared from our modern world. Today, value-neutral schools dominate our public educational systems, and cutthroat, bottom-line management principles dominate the business world.

We are in desperate need of men who live by principles, ethics, and a moral sensitivity. A truly mature, balanced man will never, for the sake of convenience or personal advancement, abandon his convictions and beliefs. A man's spiritual and personal beliefs should be the core and foundation of his strength and masculine power. After all, a man's true strength does not come from outer power but from inner conviction and truths.

Historically, the most influential men in history have been those who stood by their principles, living and teaching an ethical way of life by their actions. We think of Gandhi confronting the British in India in the early twentieth century, of Martin Luther King Jr. facing down racism and prejudice in the 1960s. The power of their principles won long-term major victories, though their immediate "battles" may not have.

At the core of a man's integrity and ethics, you will almost always find a man's faith and spirituality. Ethics and morality flow naturally from active belief in God, a background of religious upbringing and study, and a sincere prayer life. Perhaps a quote from Paul's Letter to the Philippians sums this up best:

> Finally, beloved, whatever is true, whatever is honorable, whatever is just, whatever is pure, whatever is pleasing, whatever is commendable, if there is any excellence and if there is anything worthy of praise, think about these things. Keep on doing the things that you have learned and received and heard and seen in me, and the God of peace will be with you. (Philippians 4:8–9)

Cowardice asks the question: Is it safe?
Consensus asks the question: Is it popular?
Conscience asks: Is it right?"
                    Martin Luther King Jr.

3. Honesty and openness in dealing with oneself and one's grief. There is little denial, repression, or avoidance, but rather honest confrontation of grief. Instead of "game playing," where we pretend we are stoic, stonelike, and completely untouched by our wounds, we can acknowledge our woundedness and openly admit the "earthen vessel" nature of our being. This openness with our grief may include even the shedding of tears, or the showing of long-hidden emotions, or other healing responses that may not be traditionally "masculine." Certainly it includes self-honesty.

Terry Smith's attitude expresses this well, as seen in his journal comments about adjustments he had to make following the amputation of his leg:

> I was very seldom conscious of the fact that I was changed, but I know others were. I did what I am, for the most part, in every situation. . . . I didn't go through a big deal when I was told I was to die; my biggest ordeal was learning to walk again with an artificial limb! . . . The main burden of accepting the fact that I had lost that leg rested on those dear to me.

Great men have a healthy respect for self, yet an ability to not take themselves too seriously. Thus, they can honestly admit their weaknesses, failures, even their neediness and emotional brokenness, yet move forward to confront and learn from these griefs of life.

The great thing is to get the true picture, whatever it is.
Winston Churchill, during World War II

4. Willingness to take action when needed. Many men prefer to complain or simply to sit in their weakness or brokenness. There is a strong tendency in today's culture to numb our pains with booze, drugs, or sex. The key question is not *whether* men have griefs or problems, but rather *what a man is willing to do* to confront those griefs.

A man of wisdom and integrity is willing to take constructive action in the face of personal trials, even if those actions are immensely challenging or trying. Whether it be seeking counseling or the advice of another, reading or reflecting on the topic, or whatever, a willingness to act and move forward in a potentially healing fashion is a key attribute for greatness. I feel that twelve- step programs such as Alcoholics Anonymous and others that follow that model are examples of this courageous action at its best.

When a man confronts the tremendous grief of his powerlessness over a substance such as alcohol, it is an intensely painful situation. Accepting the harsh reality of the need for change, entering into a humbling yet healing group like A.A., and then "getting with the program" faithfully—in my opinion, this is intrinsic masculine energy at its best. It is courageous, bold, humble, honest, and stronger because of its "wounding" than it could ever have been before.

I am convinced that life is 10% what happens to us, and 90% how we react to it.

                                                        Charles Swindoll

---

Closing insight

When a man of integrity, balance, and wisdom finally nears the end of his days here on earth, his own death (the ultimate grief process) is not something to be feared. Though few men care to reflect on their final days, it stands to reason that like most other

things in life, there is a proper way to prepare oneself for even that
great event.

Perhaps Martin Luther King Jr. understood this as well as any
man who ever lived. In an April 1968 speech in Memphis, one
day before he died by an assassin's bullet, his spoken words reveal
his prepared spirit.

> Like anyone, I would like to live a long life. But I am not
> concerned about that now. I just want to do God's will. And
> he's allowed me to go up to the mountain . . . and I'm hap-
> py tonight. I'm not worried about anything. I'm not fearing
> any man. Mine eyes have seen the glory of the coming of the
> Lord.

John Robinson, in his excellent book *Death of a Hero, Birth
of the Soul,* offers a closing portrait of what an enlightened man
might do to prepare for that inevitable day.

---

*The journey . . . for a man requires the one last crisis of bodily
death. Again the maturational competencies he has developed prepare him for this final passage. He can relax, for having known the
imminent divine, he knows it will receive him unconditionally and
that the paradigm of death and re-birth is more than metaphor.
When death finally arrives, it is anti-climactic, for he is no longer
afraid. He knows this parting of the curtain will open to something
else he intuited all along. He will awaken somewhere else; he will
be coming home. Thus the enlightened man dies with a smile.
. . . . His consciousness carries him across the threshold into the
other world he has been sensing all along. As always, a man will
only understand when he arrives.*

John Robinson, Death of a Hero, Birth of the Soul

Notes

1. Robert J. C. Miller and Stephen J. Hrycyniak, "Asking the Hard Questions," *Finding Your Place in the Universe* (St. Meinrad, Indiana: Abbey Press, 1995).

2. Thomas Golden, in his booklet *Gender and Cultural Differences in Grief*, makes this distinction. As mentioned earlier in this book, Golden notes that women have the tendency to be relational (living in a network of support, seeking connection with peers), and thus their key-word is *intimacy*. Men have the tendency to be hierarchical in nature, viewing the world in terms of who is governing whom. Their keyword is *independence*. See also *You Just Don't Understand*, by Deborah Tannen (Morrow Publishing, 1990).

CHAPTER TWELVE

Resources, reflections, and activities for men in pain

In this final chapter, we offer some concrete and practical resources for healing and hope in your own unique griefquest jour-
neys. We make no attempt to pass these off as our own—rather,
like the entire style of this book, they bring a small taste of a great
variety of insights from many men of differing ages, philosophies,
styles, and backgrounds who are dealing with their own inner issues. Some of these you may have seen before; some may be new
to you. But whether new or old, we pray that these resources are
helpful as you walk through your own grief and search for the light
of healing.

May your griefquest through this time of darkness be full of
hope, love, faith, and insight—with no shortage of friends!

---

*We are afflicted in every way, but not crushed; perplexed, but not
driven to despair; persecuted, but not forsaken; struck down, but
not destroyed; always carrying in the body the death of Jesus, so
that the life of Jesus may also be made visible in our bodies.*

2 Corinthians 4:8–10

Exercises for men who are griefquesting

1. Naming our losses. This can be helpful for men who may not know how to get in touch with what they are grieving, or who feel vague rumblings from within that they're uncomfortable with. A man can specifically "name his losses"—make a list for himself mentally or on paper—getting concrete and specific with names and descriptions of what he personally has lost in life.

Too often we try to brush off (because we are big, tough men) all of life's "inconveniences"—such as the loss of a wife of forty-seven years or a job of fourteen years. Instead, we need to declare very specifically just what it is we have lost. For example: "I miss Pat Casper. Pat wasn't my mother, father, or child; he was 'just' my friend for twenty-three years. He was Pat—funny, wonderful, absolutely unique." This kind of naming of our losses is not only okay, it is *necessary*. It forces us to bring into the open what is taken for granted on the inside. It's necessary to use the name of the one you loved and lost. Name your own special loss and come closer to peace with the reality and ramifications of it.

2. Giving ourselves a "grieving permit." Men need to look at the concrete and practical. If we could give ourselves a "grieving permit," thus "officially" allowing ourselves to grieve, cry, mourn, be "weak," even "fall apart" temporarily—maybe we could release our rigid self-images and masks enough to heal a bit.

A grief permit is akin to a driver's license, which you earn after many hours of practice and testing. We men have earned the right to grieve our losses because of (1) the terrible high price we pay for being a man in this modern culture, and (2) the impact that the person, job, event (or whatever) has had in our life and the depth of our grief.

3. Burning ceremonies. The action of burning can be a symbolic gesture to help us reach closure after a personal loss. In the physical act of lighting something on fire, one "lets go" of something forever, and allows himself to *release* what he has been holding onto. Yet in burning, the object is changed into ashes, to become one again with the other elemental atoms of the earth; it is not truly lost or gone. Appropriately, the action of burning signifies both *ending* and *transformation*.

One man had a long-standing relationship with his girlfriend, which she broke off abruptly when she decided she "wanted more." After several months of depression and sadness, he finally was able to burn numerous letters and papers she had given him through the years. The act of slowly burning these papers was a great act of release for him, helping to bring closure to his grief and preparing him to move on with his life.

4. Ritual tree planting. In the October 1993 issue of *Bereavement* magazine, Rabbi Arthur Schaefer shares the beautiful Jewish practice of Ritual Tree Planting. In Jewish tradition, the ritual involves the planting of a new tree, then telling a story about the person's life whom the tree commemorates, and finally reciting the traditional Jewish prayer of mourning called the *Kaddish*.

This Jewish practice, based on an old rabbinic story and tradition from generations ago, continues today. (Witness the popular movie *Schindler's List*, in which a tree was planted for Oscar Schindler in Israel in memory of what he did for Jews during the war.) With adaptations, this ritual could be a powerful one for men to use in their own griefquesting.

Developing a daily prayer life

Beginning a prayer life is a very personal thing—it can be as simple or complicated, as long or short as you choose to make it. Allow me to suggest one simple method for beginning to pray that uses several basic steps:

1. Set aside time daily. This can be a regular time at home before or after work, right after rising (while sipping coffee?), before bedtime; or it could be during a work break; or even while traveling on the way to work. The key is to put aside some set time (at *least* several minutes) daily for you and God.

2. Thank and praise God. All prayer should start off with words of thanks to God from whom all things come. Run through a mental list of all the blessings you have to be grateful for, speak your gratitude, and praise God for his glory and power.

3. Read or listen to the Scriptures (if possible). If you have time to read passages from the Bible itself, great. But more and more people are using Scriptures on tape (in the car on the way to work, for example), daily meditation or reflection books (one Scripture passage or thought for a day), or listening to Christian music on tape or radio. Whatever we do, believers need to be fed from the Word of Life regularly in order to grow and flourish in faith and spirituality. Public worship at church does not alone suffice!

4. Meditate and reflect. After taking in God's words or insights, try to sit quietly before the Lord to listen, meditate, reflect, or hear what God has to say. Allow what you have heard to sink into your soul and spirit. What message can you take for your day from this?

5. Speak your prayers to God. Finally, speak back to God in prayer. Formal prayers such as the Our Father are helpful, but do not hesitate to speak in your own words from your heart. Use the *ACTS formula* to guide your words: ADORE God by telling him you love him. CONFESS your weakness and sins to God honestly, asking for forgiveness and strength. THANK and praise God again. Last, ask or SUPPLICATE God humbly, bringing him your needs, concerns, and worries, as well as those of the larger world and community.

Words of hope from the Scriptures

There is perhaps no better place of comfort and rest for men dealing with grief than the eternal wisdom of the Scriptures. The words and messages are timeless, though written generations ago. Men may have their own favorite passages, which I strongly encourage them to use frequently as "food for the day." But here are a few other passages that deal with issues of grief, loss, frustration, pain, fear, death, and the like. I encourage you to read each one slowly and meditatively, pausing as often and as long as needed to draw out the depth of insight each passage may have for you personally.

◆ Psalm 23 (the classic prayer of trust in God)
◆ Psalm 77 (comfort in times of great distress)
◆ Psalm 139 (God knows my heart and my entire journey)
◆ Isaiah 43:1–4 (do not fear—you are precious in my sight)
◆ Jeremiah 17:5–8 (true wisdom = trusting God, not human beings)
◆ Matthew 5—7 (basic blueprint for faith-filled living in integrity)
◆ Luke 12:13–34 (trust in God, not in things of the earth)
◆ Romans 8:18–39 (the Spirit of God helps us in weakness and trial)
◆ 1 Corinthians 15:51–57 ("Where, O death, is your victory?")

A Scripture-based meditation for men

Read Luke 6:6–11. It is the story of a man with a withered arm. Richard Rohr, OFM, calls this story the "prototypical example of 'wounded men' in today's world." (See Rohr's tape series *A Man's Approach to God.*) The story is a fertile source of meditation, reflecting three levels of men. Where do you fit in?

1. Man with withered arm—a man whose power is weakened. (The right arm being withered is a symbol of a man's "powerful side" being weakened.) This represents men who are "soft," who have capitulated to the world's values and thus given up their real power, who are caught in the "wrong" issues, whose life priorities are imbalanced.

2. Scribes, Pharisees, religious leaders of the day—symbolic of men who are lost in the backwaters of trivial issues (for example, religious legalism, workaholism, and so on), who are out of contact with the larger issues of life—personal faith, family, integrity.

3. Jesus Christ—the paradigm for the healthy balanced male, the man who confronts injustice and narrow-mindedness here and elsewhere and brings healing and freedom to "wounded men" everywhere. This is the ideal man we need to touch for healing!

Remembering loved ones at holidays

Holidays can be times of great anxiety, stress, and loneliness when you have lost a loved one. Creating some new rituals and traditions that memorialize the lost one may be helpful. For example:

- Decorate a wreath or tree with pictures and items that were special to the person. You might want to place the wreath at the gravesite.
- Make a book of pictures or memorabilia of the lost one to give to or simply share with loved ones. This can be especially helpful for children.
- Make a donation to a favorite charity in the person's honor.
- Wrap a favorite keepsake or framed picture of the deceased, and give it as a gift to another grieving family member.
- Bring your loved one's favorite food to share at a holiday dinner. Mention his or her name in the blessing over the food, or propose a toast in memory.
- Share anecdotes and favorite stories about the person who died. Sometimes others need permission to talk about a deceased loved one. Let them know you would rather keep the memory alive than pretend nothing has happened.

Using "The Cardinal Rules of Crisis"
(See Appendix Two)

There come times in a person's life when the entire world has apparently collapsed, and it seems there is nowhere to go. When a crisis shatters our world, or we get stuck in a dark pit of grief, we may completely lose our sense of perspective. We don't know where to go, what to do, how to get along. It is for times like these—times of total confusion, depression, despondency, or brokenness—that "The Cardinal Rules of Crisis" are intended.

These rules were born in 1989, perhaps the single roughest year of my own life. I had taken a leave from the priesthood, was unsure about my future, and was confused about my purpose in life. It was a midlife time of questing, searching, and grieving without knowing for what. In attempting to keep balance within myself, and to find God in the desert of those months, I created these eight essential guidelines for survival. I read them and reflected on them daily, sometimes several times a day. The God-inspired wisdom they contain helped keep me focused on the unchanging priorities of life—my own essential goodness and value, the love of a God always with me, and the new life that would emerge despite the temporary pain of the present. I offer them to you now. If you are at a place of great pain or personal turmoil, of intense loneliness or deep grief, I encourage you to use them. You might want to use them as follows:

1. Read them daily, or as often as you feel overwhelmed by your pain. They can be an anchor holding you fast against the surging tides of depression, loneliness, or pain. Sit quietly as you do so.

2. Meditate on them slowly, one by one. Do not rush through them. Allow the words of each rule to sink into the part of your being where the confusion and turmoil is the worst.

3. Reflect on the wisdom they contain. Spend several moments contemplating the lesson contained in each rule. Each of them reflects a truth that is unchanged by your temporary emotional state.

4. Offer a prayer to God, in whatever words or way you want. The Power that is God can be addressed in many ways. All that is important is to enter into a personal, private moment with the Supreme Being and express your heart's feelings and desires. Allow yourself to rest for a moment in the arms of that gentle Being who, despite whatever has happened, will never abandon you. You and God—God in you—that's all that's important in the end.

Throughout the generations, poets have struggled to put into words the feelings so powerfully present within the human heart. Some poetry and literature written by men poignantly expresses the pain and searching of the male griefquest. Due to limitations of space, we cannot provide the actual poetry here, but we have listed several selections that may be helpful to your griefquest.

John Robinson, in his excellent book *Death of a Hero, Birth of the Soul*, includes many fine poems that powerfully capture the movements of a man through moments of grief, loss, and love. Some of Robinson's selections include:

◆ Carl Sandburg, "The People, Yes" (p. 155)
◆ Walt Whitman, "Song of Myself" (pp. 237–239)
◆ Theodore Roethke, "Lost Son" (p. 188)
◆ D. H. Lawrence, "The Primal Passions" (p. 161), "Healing" (p. 173)
◆ Rainer Maria Rilke, "Autumn" (p. 110), "The Man Watching" (p. 169)
◆ Stanley Kunitz, "End of Summer" (p. 106)

The famous Spanish mystic and saint John of the Cross wrote a particularly powerful description of the way to knowledge in his classic *Ascent of Mt. Carmel*. It can be found in Book I, 13, number 10 of that spiritual classic.

Alfred Lord Tennyson is the author of the legendary *Idylls of the King*. The section entitled "The Passing of Arthur," which tells of the knight Bedivere's dealing with the death of the great King Arthur, is especially poignant.

Bibliography

Articles

Harper, Jeanne M., MPS. "Men and Grief." *Griefnet* (Internet), Alpha-Omega Venture, 1113 Elizabeth Ave., P. O. Box 735, Marinette, WI 54143-0755.

Parachin, Victor. "Grief Relief." *Catholic Cemetery* (November 1995), pp. 33–34.

Audiocassette series

Rohr, Richard. *A Man's Approach to God.* Cincinnati: St. Anthony Messenger Press, 1989.

Booklets or pamphlets

Golden, Thomas. *A Man's Grief* (1994); *Different Paths Toward Healing* (1994); *Gender and Cultural Differences in Grief* (1994). 10400 Connecticut Ave., Suite 514, Kensington, MD 20895. For information regarding publications or workshops, call 301-942-9192; e-mail *tgolden@dgsys.com*; URL: *http://www2.dgsys./~tgolden/1grief.html.*

Helping Men in Grief. Colorado Springs, CO: Bereavement Publishing, 1992.

Parachin, Victor. *The Lord Is My Shepherd.* Liguori, MO: Liguori Publications, 1992.

Rabior, The Reverend W. *Surviving Life's Losses.* Liguori, MO: Liguori Publications, 1994.

161

Books

Arnold, Patrick. *Wildmen, Warriors and Kings*. New York: Crossroad, 1991.

Byrd, Dennis. *Rise and Walk*. Grand Rapids, MI: Zondervan, 1993.

Carroll, L. Patrick, and Katherine Marie Dyckman. *Chaos or Creation: Spirituality in Mid-Life*. Mahwah, NJ: Paulist Press, 1986.

Farmer, Steven. *The Wounded Male*. New York: Ballantine, 1991.

Fulghum, Robert. *From Beginning to End*. New York: Villard Publishing, 1995.

Gray, John. *Men Are from Mars, Women Are from Venus*. New York: HarperCollins, 1992.

Johnson, Robert. *He: Understanding Masculine Psychology*. New York: Harper and Row, 1989.

Jung, Carl. *Modern Man in Search of a Soul*. New York: Harvest Books, 1933.

Oates, Wayne. *Your Particular Grief*. Louisville, KY: Westminster/John Knox Press, 1981.

Parachin, Victor. *Our Father: A Prayer for the Grieving*. Liguori, MO: Liguori Publishing, 1993.

Robertson, John. *Death of a Hero, Birth of the Soul*. Sacramento, CA: Tzedakah Publishing, 1995.

Rohr, Richard. *Quest for the Grail*. New York: Crossroad, 1994.

Sanford, John. *Healing and Wholeness*. Mahwah, NJ: Paulist Press, 1977.

———. *The Kingdom Within*. Mahwah, NJ: Paulist Press, 1970.

Smith, David. *The Friendless American Male*. Ventura, CA: Regal Books, 1983.

Staudacher, Carol. *Men and Grief*. Oakland, CA: New Harbinger Press, 1991.

Westberg, Granger. *Good Grief*. Minneapolis: Fortress Press, 1971.

Publishers

Bereavement Publishing, 8133 Telegraph Drive, Colorado Springs, CO 80920, 719-282-1948. Publisher of *Bereavement*, a magazine offering hope and healing for those who have lost a loved one. Features articles, poems, memorials, counseling, resources.

One Caring Place, Abbey Press, St. Meinrad, IN 47577, 800-325-2511. Publishes CareNotes, PrayerNotes, CareNotes for Teens, Consolations Books, Elf-Help Books, What Helps the Most Books, and Wisdom of the Heart Books—on grief and a wide variety of other critical issues.

The Rainbow Connection, 477 Hannah Branch Road, Burnsville, NC 28714, 704-675-5909. Offers a fine line of grief-related resources: books, tapes, candles, and so on.

Support group

The Compassionate Friends, P. O. Box 3696, Oak Brook, IL 60522-3696, 708-990-0010. A national support group that allows parents to share their grief over the death of a child.

Grief-related resources and speakers

The World Pastoral Care Center, Rev. Richard B. Gilbert, 1504 North Campbell Street, Valparaiso, IN 46385-3454, 219-464-8183. Reverend Gilbert has compiled a resource center of speakers, articles, books, and programs highlighting every aspect of grieving and loss. There is no better place to begin or to deepen your knowledge of the griefquest process than this invaluable center.

The Cardinal Rules of Crisis

In case of crisis, read this first!

When life seems overwhelming . . . when nothing else around you seems to work . . . when grief, loss, loneliness, fear, worry, anger, or any other negative emotion seems to be washing over you like an uncontrollable flood . . . then it is the time to remember . . .

The Cardinal Rules of Crisis

1. **You will survive despite your pain.** All feelings are transitory and will pass.

2. **Self-hatred is a lie.** Self-pity is ultimately useless. Do not wallow in them.

3. **You are still beloved, valuable, and worthwhile in God's eyes,** despite what you feel about yourself. Your dignity and self-worth are unchanged by outer circumstances.

4. **Your pain has been seen and redeemed by Jesus Christ on the cross.** "I can do all things through him who strengthens me" (Philippians 4:13).

5. **One day at a time!** One hour at a time! One *minute* at a time if need be!

6. **Postpone any important life decisions until later.** Wait until the sense of loss or pain lifts a bit.

7. **Structure helps maintain sanity.** Though it may seem flat, dull, and empty, continue with your work and your personal daily routine. Keep on keepin' on! Hope will triumph in the end!

8. **Reach out to friends and loved ones.** Every burden in the world becomes lighter when carried with a friend.

About the authors

Bob Miller was born in Grand Rapids, Michigan, and ordained to the priesthood in 1976. After twenty years of religious life with the Redemptorists, he recently joined the archdiocese of Chicago and now ministers in Chicago's southside black community, where he is co-pastor at Holy Angels Church. He has preached parish missions and renewals, has worked with Marriage Encounter and charismatic renewal, and has done varied retreat work. He is co-author of the Abbey Press book *Finding Your Place in the Universe*.

Stephen J. Hrycyniak is an ordained deacon in the Ukrainian Greek Catholic Church and serves as the executive director of Theological Book Services. He resides in Franklin, Wisconsin, with his wife and four children.